Self-Management – Understanding, Communicating, and Assessing Behavioral Competency, 3rd Edition

For permission requests contact the author:
Gian Paolo Roma
romag@sunybroome.edu

Gian Paolo Roma
SUNY Broome Community College
PO Box 1017
Binghamton, NY 13902

CreateSpace.com Self-Publishing Group
Self-Management – Understanding, Communicating, and Assessing Behavioral Competency
Gian Paolo Roma

ISBN-13: 978 1070825465
ISBN-10: 1070825468

Printed in the United States of America.

Cover Design by Gian Paolo Roma
Cover Art by the late Kari Ellen Bonini-Roma
Cover Photography by: Corinne Roma
Cover Fonts: IrisUPC & Calibri
Interior Design by Gian Paolo Roma
Interior Font: Times Roman

Self-Management

Understanding, Communicating, and Assessing Behavioral Competency

Third Edition

Gian Paolo Roma

Dedications

"You are rewarding a teacher poorly if you remain always a pupil."

~ Friedrich Nietzsche

To my greatest teachers Arlene, Alli, and Cori.

I am indebted to the following reviewers who have been so generous with their time, advice, input, encouragement, expertise, and experience.

Dawne Adams, MS
Binghamton High School
Associate Principle

John Bunnell, MBA
SUNY Broome Community College
Business Department

Gina Chase, MS
SUNY Broome Community College
Applied Learning Career Specialist

Erin Frye, MBA
SUNY Broome Community College
Business Department

William R. Hollister, PhD
SUNY Broome Community College
Biology Department

Annette LeRoy, AAS
SUNY Broome Community College
BPS Division

Meghan McGuinness, EdD
SUNY Broome Community College
Professor-Dental Hygiene Department

Dina Naples-Layish, PhD
Binghamton University
School of Management

Charles Petrolawicz, JD, MBA
SUNY Broome Community College
Professor-Business Department

Andrea Roma, MS
SUNY Broome Community College
Fast Forward/Early College/P-Tech/Articulations

Leslie Scalzo, AA
SUNY Broome Community College
BPS Division

Nicole Tryt, MS
Broome-Tioga BOCES
Assistant Principle

Ed Yetsko, MBA
SUNY Broome Community College
Business Department

Francis Battisti, PhD
SUNY Broome Community College
Chief Academic Officer

Lauren Bunnell, MA
SUNY Broome Community College
BPS Division

Katherine Collette, MSW
Binghamton University
School of Management

Brenda Gainer, PhD
York University
Schulich School of Business

Robert Hurley, PhD
Fordham University
Gabelli School of Business

Brian Loy, MA, JD
SUNY Broome Community College
Business Department

Beth Mollen, MBA
SUNY Broome Community College
VP and Dean PBS Division

Diane O'Heron, PhD
SUNY Broome Community College
English Department

Leslie Reid, MS
SUNY Broome Community College
Staff Associate - BPS Division

Jenna M. Rosenberg, MBA, SPHR
Visions Federal Credit Union
Human Resources Department

Mary Seel, MA
SUNY Broome Community College
English Department

Kerry Weber, MA
SUNY Broome Community College
Criminal Justice & Emergency Service Department

Ellen Brand, PhD
SUNY Broome Community College
English Department

Irene Byrnes, MA
SUNY Broome Community College
Philosophy Department

Jack Duffy, PhD
Dalhousie University
Rowe School of Business

D. Lee Heron, PhD
SUNY Broome Community College
Business Department

Michael Kuryla, MS
SUNY Broome Community College
Business Department

Gerald Loy, JD
SUNY Broome Community College
Business Department

Mark Mushalla, CPA
SUNY Broome Community College
Business Department

Stephen Ohl, MBA, CPM, CPSM
SUNY Broome Community College
Professor-Business Department

Alexandra Roma, MEd
Chenango Forks High School
English Teacher

Mark Ryan, MBA
SUNY Broome Community College
Business Information Technology Department

Andrea Sollitto, MST
SUNY Broome Community College
BPS Division

Rey Wojdat, EdD
SUNY Broome Community College
Hospitality Department

Table of Contents

A brief discussion of the rationale and philosophy of self-management.

Unit 1 Overview

A summary of a comprehensive, rational, and applied self-management methodology.

Unit 2 Communication

A rational and applied system of thinking for understanding and assessing communication-based trust relating to message appropriateness and effectiveness; and introduction of the A.I.M.E. Communication Methodology.

Introduction

Introduction

"People pay for what they do, and still more for what they have allowed themselves to become. And they pay for it very simply: by the lives they lead."

~ James Baldwin

Ideally, human behavior that is governed by reason follows a predictable order of related things. Desires beget feelings, feelings beget thoughts, thoughts beget choices, choices beget character, character begets relationships, and relationships beget results. In a reason-based world, thoughts are organized *before* choices involving actions and words are made.

Reason-Based Behavior Cycle

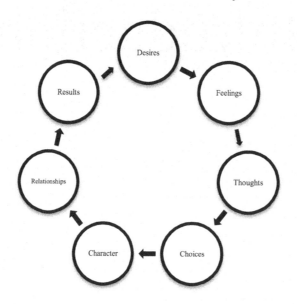

But when we are young or when our choices are not governed by reason, we may bypass thinking altogether and make impulsive choices based primarily on our desires and feelings. For example, infants are all impulse. They act and react based on the feelings in their bodies without considering consequences. They "coo" when they are happy; they cry when they are uncomfortable. Infants go to the bathroom in their diapers because their *feelings* control their choices. Infants do not think about where and when it is appropriate to relieve themselves.

As we mature, we hopefully become more aware of how our desires and feelings influence our choices. We begin to comprehend cause and effect. Over time we create *rules* for ourselves that govern our conduct because we begin to understand the notion that our behaviors have consequences not only for ourselves but also for others. We may even begin to realize that if we go about our daily lives without a system of rules to guide our own thinking and conduct, it may become increasingly difficult to enjoy interacting with others because unmanaged behavior can create conflict.

Behavioral rules can be defined as ….

Unambiguous rules that govern an individual's behavior within particular contexts involving others.

Rules governing behavior (i.e. values, ethics, codes of conduct, personal policies) would not be necessary if there were only one human being that lived his or her life without social contact with others. The only person that could be harmed by the choices of an individual existing in complete isolation is oneself. Although obvious, it is precisely because of others that rules governing individual conduct are so necessary. Behavioral rules are necessary because of our unending struggle to fulfill our own desires within contexts involving others.

Games are contexts (or social environments) in which individuals interact with one another. All games have rules. The rules are the structure within which players interact. Games require that players understand and willingly follow a set of rules so that everyone can enjoy interacting and do so without too much conflict. If all of the players easily weaved together their competing desires in a fair and just manner when they interacted, then there would be no need for rules. It is precisely because some players do not manage their desires well when they interact socially with others that rules are required. In many games, such as basketball or ice hockey, players that knowingly or unknowingly violate the rules too many times foul out of the game. Players who foul out effectively take *themselves* out of the game and are no longer able to enjoy playing the game with others.

All rules that govern human interactions must be fair, understood, and, most importantly, agreed upon by everyone. Rules help societies (i.e. families, schools, communities, work places, cities, and countries) manage individual desires within contexts involving others. In a larger sense, all rules of conduct are man-made social constructs or norms that help societies weave together the competing desires of individuals so that everyone can enjoy the benefits associated with interacting socially with everyone else without too much conflict.

Rules of conduct are social formulas that govern behavior and make it possible for different-minded individuals to interact in a socially like-minded manner.

Behavioral rules create the framework within which society manages individual desires in the *Game of Life*. If an individual genuinely does not want to foul out in the game of life (in school, work, or with family and friends), the individual should understand and then organize his or her own desires, thoughts, choices, and behaviors so that both the individual's desires and the desires of everyone else can be successfully woven together.

To understand and organize one's own desires, one must be able to comprehend and accept the notion that multiple desires exist simultaneously and compete for dominance within everyone. One must also be able to grasp the idea that one's own choice of desires can simultaneously impact reality for oneself and others. For example, one can simultaneously desire to smoke cigarettes but at the very same time, also desire good health for oneself and others. The idea that smoking cigarettes is related to good health is removed from reality by something more than a respectful distance. Yet, the United States Department of Health and Human Services reports that "since 1964 approximately 2,500,000 nonsmokers have died from health problems caused by exposure to secondhand smoke."[1] Each time a smoker chooses to light up around others, he or she simultaneously increases the risk of serious health problems or death, not only for the smoker but also for those around the smoker.

The degree of concern one has for oneself is always in a context involving others. Although it can be rightly argued that an individual must have the right to pursue one's own life, liberty, and happiness, doing so without understanding and following rules is irresponsible for the individual and society. So, if individuals and societies can accept the notions that desires compete for dominance within all people and that organizing and prioritizing our desires is a good idea for individuals and society as a whole, then it makes sense to organize a system of thinking around these things.

The main reason that individuals should study things like one's own desires, values, thinking, choices, and behavior is to get one's system of thinking in order so that one can anticipate and avoid many of the struggles that one might walk into head first if one walked through life blindly. The main purpose of this book is to help students achieve their goals by clarifying the behaviors that they alone are responsible for, showing why they are important, and how they lead to success.

This book introduces a comprehensive self-management model to help students understand and assess their own behavioral performance. The book provides a practical framework, how to exercises, a new behavioral observation measurement system, behavioral profile, self-tests, and a behavioral change methodology for individuals, families, and schools seeking to establish, assess, and improve behavioral performance.

---

1. U.S. Department of Health and Human Services. The Health Consequences of Smoking—50 Years of Progress: A Report of the Surgeon General. Atlanta: U.S. Department of Health and Human Services, Centers for Disease Control and Prevention, National Center for Chronic Disease Prevention and Health Promotion, Office on Smoking and Health, 2014 [accessed 2017 Feb 21].

Professor Roma can be reached at romag@sunybroome.edu. He gets many emails and will try to respond to yours as quickly as he can. He usually doesn't answer calls from unrecognized phone numbers, so please leave a message if he doesn't answer, and he will call you back as soon as he is able.

Mr. Gian Paolo Roma
Professor and Chair of the Business Programs Department
SUNY Broome Community College
PO Box 1017
Binghamton, NY 13902

Office: (607) 778-5133

Unit 1

Overview

Self-Management:
Understanding, Communicating and Assessing
Behavioral Competency, 3rd Edition
Gian Paolo Roma - © 2019 - All Rights Reserved

Overview

"The first and best victory is to conquer self."

~ Plato

Rules governing behavior (i.e. values, ethics, codes of conduct, personal policies) would not be necessary if there were only one human being that lived his or her life without social contact with others. The only person that could be harmed by the choices of an individual existing in complete insolation is oneself. Although obvious, it is precisely because of *others* that rules governing individual conduct are so necessary. Behavioral rules are necessary *because* of our unending struggle to fulfill our own desires within contexts involving others. Others not only include people who think, act, believe, and look like you, but also people who do not. A partial list of others may include women, men, teachers, classmates, co-workers, bosses, republicans, democrats, independents, liberals, conservatives, moderates, social democrats, libertarians, Jews, Muslims, Hindus, Buddhists, Christians, atheists, agnostics, Canadians, French, English, Germans, Syrians, Mexicans, North Koreans, South Koreans, Iranians, Russians, Chinese, Blacks, Latinos, Asians, LGBTQs, heterosexuals, coaches, teammates, neighbors, immigrants, police, union and nonunion members, family, friends, foes, pro-life, pro-choice, motorists, pedestrians. As of the printing of this book, almost 8 billion others inhabit this world with you.

How can you better prepare yourself to be more resilient, prepared, and effective at reaching your goals in this increasingly diverse, demanding, changing, and competitive world involving so many others? One way is to learn and practice the basic behaviors that are necessary to achieve goals. We can define behavior as ….

a type of person, doing an action, in a specific context.[2]

Your success and achievement, be it academic, social, career, financial, or otherwise, will primarily be a function of your own behavior. You will have a larger impact on your future than your parents, siblings, friends, schools, religion, government, and employers. That's because you are responsible for directing the course of your life.

You are responsible for you.

---

[2] Fogg, BJ, Stanford University, Behavior By Design: *New Models of Behavior and New Methods for Design Lecture*, Website: http://www.bjfogg.org.

True self-confidence and genuine competence are *outcomes* of sustained efforts made over long periods to achieve goals and cannot be inherited or acquired by those unwilling to endure the rigors of life. Although others can help you formulate plans on how best to achieve your goals, ultimately *you* are the only person that can turn your plans into reality.

Behavioral competency can be characterized as a basic understanding and consistent practice of a set of skills that nurtures trust.

Trust is having *confident reliance* in others in situations involving vulnerability or risk.[3] Behaviorally competent people comprehend how their own behavior affects trust. They have an emotional and intellectual appreciation of the role trust plays in goal achievement and a willingness to consider how their own actions and words affect trust. Trust is the outcome of responsible behavior. A simple definition of Self-Management (SM) is …

the ability to achieve one's own goals in a trustworthy manner.

We can think in the abstract of individual behavior as either *strengthening* or *weakening* trust - or *healthy* or *unhealthy,* respectively. *Healthy behaviors* are defined as those that are responsible, strengthen trust connections, and create goodwill between people. Examples of healthy behaviors are showing up on time, working hard, appreciating others, and effectively adapting to difficult or changing situations. *Unhealthy behaviors* or irresponsible behaviors such as lack of effort, being unreliable, disrespecting others, using poor judgment, and making reckless decisions, can cause others to feel upset, frustrated, scared, and angry, which can destroy goodwill and cooperation between people.

Unhealthy behaviors may require other people (e.g. supervisors, professors, parents, advisors, family-members, police) to intervene to prevent negative outcomes from occurring. In the United States our founders created an entire branch of government to manage unlawful behavior. People that are convicted of legal wrongdoing can be forced to live behind bars for years (even their entire lives), unable to interact with the outside world because they cannot be trusted to manage their own affairs without hurting themselves or others. The most extreme examples of behavioral intervention are jail and the death penalty, but lesser degrees of unhealthy behavior also erode trust among law-abiding citizens.

Ultimately, the only thing that people have with others are relationships. The same is true for organizations in which people interact such as schools, hospitals, partnerships, corporations, not-

---

[3] Hurley, Robert, "The Decision to Trust: How Leaders Create High Trust Organizations", *Jossey-Bass*, 2011, p.25.

for-profits, small businesses, and government entities. Again, the only thing that these organizations have with their people are relationships. Relationships between people and within organizations can be good or bad and depend on the way people interact with each other. Without trust it is difficult to build healthy relations with others because people do not *willingly* interact with people they do not trust. Because trust is the cornerstone of all healthy relationships, it is necessary and appropriate to study and understand what trust is and how it is built. Behaviors make visible what is trustworthy and untrustworthy about a person's character. SM requires that people organize and control their own behavioral reactions through self-imposed, trustworthy rules of conduct or personal policies.

> ***Self-management focuses on understanding and then continuously improving one's own emotional, intellectual, and physical reactions to life's events.***

The behaviors discussed in this book are called the 5Cs of SM and can be self-cultivated, self-assessed, and self-managed by almost anyone. The 5Cs are individual responsibilities that every person must manage within himself or herself and cannot be delegated to others. The 5Cs are communication, choice, commitment, coping, and caring (Figure 1). Simply put, everyone is responsible for how they communicate, how they make choices, how caring they are to others, how committed they are to the activities they are involved with, and how well they cope with the challenges in their lives. These behavioral responsibilities cannot be outsourced to others.

5Cs of Self-Management Model

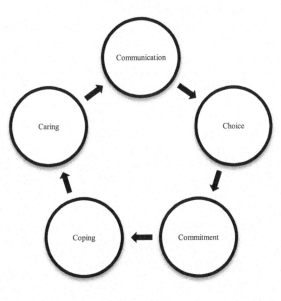

Figure 1

Self-Management:
Understanding, Communicating and Assessing
Behavioral Competency, 3rd Edition
Gian Paolo Roma - © 2019 - All Rights Reserved

The core mission of this book is to create a more trusting society by clarifying how the 5Cs relate to trust and providing *how to* help in applying them to life. The 5Cs are multifaceted and transmit different character traits that are linked to specific types of trust. Simply put, a person can be trustworthy in one of the 5C dimensions but not another. For example, it is entirely possible for an individual to be committed to a job or college, but not care about the people that she or he works or goes to school with. Likewise, it is also possible for an individual to commit to one activity, cope with one situation, care about one person, make a good choice in one situation, or communicate appropriately to some people *but not others*.

Most importantly, the 5Cs can be used to identify, diagnose, and evaluate *trustworthiness* and *behavioral* performance. Each of the 5Cs has a specific trust dimension and a clearly defined trust definition that describes the standard of behavior that is expected for each of the 5Cs. (see Table 1.1).

<u>5Cs of SM</u>	<u>Trust Dimension</u>	<u>Trust Definition</u>
Communication	Communication-Based	Trust a person to convey messages appropriately to others.
Choices	Judgment-Based	Trust a person to prioritize important matters ahead of unimportant matters.
Caring	Relationship-Based	Trust a person to show thoughtful concern for others.
Commitment	Activity-Based	Trust a person to follow through and meet obligations.
Coping	Situation-Based	Trust a person to handle and adapt effectively to difficult, changing, and complex circumstances.

Table 1.1

Behavioral conduct that is contrary to the standards would, by definition, be self-defeating and undermine one's self-interest. Behaviors like communicating inappropriately, prioritizing unimportant matters ahead of important matters, failing to meet obligations to others, handling difficult situations poorly, or disrespecting others are problematic because they demonstrate poor judgment and untrustworthiness. They create *credibility gaps* that can damage relationships, and therefore, reduce one's own chances of getting ahead in life.

According to a report published in 2014, only 55% of first-time undergraduates who matriculated in the fall of 2008 finished a degree within six years.[4] This means that 45% of students who attempted college failed to graduate after six years. Although there are many factors affecting college graduation rates, such as the cost, inability to balance school, jobs and family, and academic preparedness, many students don't graduate because their own behavioral decision-making is antithetical to the 5Cs. They may not communicate appropriately or use good judgment or follow through and meet their obligations in their classes or cope well with the difficulties they encounter in college. In short, they may not graduate because they may not understand or have a palpable sense of duty about their own behavioral obligations; they may not be engaging in trustworthy and responsible behavior.

What do you think?

How do you treat people who you don't trust? Would you hire someone you didn't trust? Explain your answer.

_____

_____

_____

_____

_____

Before we continue, let's stop and define two key terms that are essential to understanding behavior: *behavioral occurrences and behavioral patterns.*

---

[4] National Student Clearinghouse Research Center Signature Report: *Completing College, A National View of Student Attainment Rates, Fall 2008 Cohort:* Online Source: https://nscresearchcenter.org/wp-content/uploads/SignatureReport8.pdf

Understanding Behavioral Occurrences and Behavioral Patterns

A behavioral occurrence is …

a one-time event or a single behavioral incident that happens.

For example, a person might be absent or late or not do their homework once for reasons that are usually not self-created. Whereas, a behavioral pattern is …

conduct that repeatedly or continually exists, is predictable, and is usually self-created.

Behavioral patterns reveal themselves after a number of behavioral occurrences have happened. For instance, frequent occurrences of rude and disrespectful behavior towards others would be indicative of an inconsiderate behavioral pattern. When assessing and diagnosing behavioral performance (in yourself or others), there are two reasons why it is important to determine if the behavior in question is an isolated behavioral occurrence or a behavioral pattern.

First, life happens. From time to time unforeseen circumstances *occur* (bad weather, car problems, illness, and personal issues). When situations occur that are the result of chance, bad luck, or divine providence, it is entirely reasonable *not* to conform to what is behaviorally expected because the motivation to act in a contrary manner is not self-created. For example, it is entirely reasonable for a person to be late or absent if he or she has a flat tire or a car accident or is in the middle of a snowstorm.

Second, human beings are not perfect; we make mistakes. Because humans are human, it's unreasonable to expect that they can operate at peak performance all of the time.[5] People make mistakes because they can be inattentive, preoccupied, bored, tired, irritable, upset, sad, hurt, depressed, worried, overly enthusiastic, scared, or overwhelmed. Emotions, feelings, and *states of mind* can cause people to be careless and act *before* they think. When normally trustworthy individuals are *thoughtless* and act in ways (intentionally or otherwise) that do not conform to their established or accepted pattern of behavior, the conduct is said to be *out-of-character*. Both chance and out-of-character occurrences are discrete events that should not happen repeatedly. When either chance or out-of-character occurrences become the norm, behavioral patterns come into view.

---

[5] Special Note: In some professions (doctors, nurses, pharmacists, members of the military, public safety professionals, lifeguards.) behavioral mistakes can cause injury or death. In these types of professions, even out-of-character occurrences may not be tolerated.

Behavioral occurrences become behavioral patterns when conduct is repeated, frequent, predictable, and self-created.

While some behavioral patterns are healthy, some are not. Some patterns are responsible and strengthen trust, while others are irresponsible and weaken trust. For example, over the course of a semester, repeated occurrences of absenteeism would be indicative of possible commitment related problems.

Sometimes behavioral patterns are difficult to see and take time to reveal themselves. The important thing to remember is that trustworthy and untrustworthy behavioral patterns exist and reveal character traits (good and bad) about each of us. Just knowing the distinction between behavioral occurrences and behavioral patterns is an important first step in understanding how to assess and improve behavioral performance. What could be more important than understanding your own behavioral patterns? One of the main goals of this book is to provide a framework within which to identify, assess, and diagnose your own behavioral performance.

Why are behavioral patterns important?

Behavioral patterns are important because they communicate how trustworthy we are to others that experience us.

A recent study published in the Harvard Business Review found that "98% of workers polled reported experiencing uncivil behavior" in the workplace[6]. This finding is significant because behaviors like incivility that undermine the dignity, confidence, and self-worth of others can weaken or possibly even sever the trust connections that bind people together. Once trust is broken, unhappiness, conflict, and polarization often result, any of which can compromise or destroy goodwill between people. Many of the biggest problems we face in society can be traced back to untrustworthy behavior that has destroyed people's willingness to cooperate with one another.

The study suggests that most people (young and old) go through life without giving any serious thought or having a depth of understanding about their own behavior and how it can affect their lives individually and our society as a whole. If 98% of people surveyed experience relationship mistrust at work, everyone's goodwill and willingness to cooperate has been compromised. How can we move forward collectively when no one trusts each other? How can this be good for us individually or the world as a whole?

---

[6] Porath, Christine, and Pearson, Christine, "The Price of Incivility", *Harvard Business Review* Jan-Feb 2013, p.114.

Continuous Behavioral Improvement Process

The continuous behavioral improvement process (CBIP) (Figure 2) is a methodology to improve the 5Cs through incremental and informed thinking about one's own behavior. CBIP relies on the individual to identify areas of behavioral improvement within him or herself because individuals know themselves better and are therefore uniquely qualified to identify and solve their own behavior-related problems.

Because CBIP relies on the individual for ideas about his or her own behavioral improvement, he or she is more invested in the behavioral outcome, which increases the chance of successful and sustainable improvement.

Continuous Behavioral Improvement Process

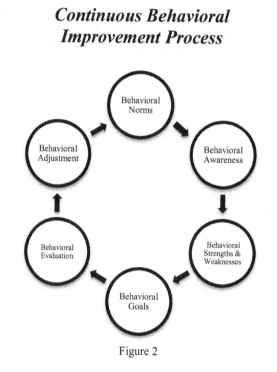

Figure 2

Behavioral Norms

In order for CBIP to work, individuals must first be willing to accept the notion that societies must have *ground rules* or behavioral norms to function properly.

> *Behavioral norms are generally accepted social qualities or characteristics that are deemed essential for successfully living together in society.*

Behavioral norms are the foundation upon which our communities and social order are built. Behavioral norms are behavioral rules that allow individuals to interact with one another without too much conflict. In the United States, we believe that individuals have the absolute *right* to pursue life, liberty, and happiness. But, it can be persuasively argued that *how* we pursue our rights to life, liberty, and happiness is as important as the rights themselves. As Lyndon Johnson famously said, "Any jackass can kick down a barn, but it takes a good carpenter to build one."[7]

It takes behavioral talent to achieve our goals without hurting others and oneself.

How individuals interact with each other is more important than *what* people actually do together. We may damage the community in which we all live, if we as individuals pursue our own life, liberty, and happiness without any ground rules, or regard for others and the behavioral norms that others expect. Being nice, working hard, or communicating appropriately are not about being *politically correct*. On the contrary, it is that doing otherwise hurts everyone. If we all drink from the same polluted water, we all suffer. How can societies function or move forward in a healthy manner if individuals *poison* the society that we all live in?

Individuals who are unwilling to adopt these norms, or are unaware of generally accepted behavioral norms, hurt themselves because their behavior is contrary to the common interests of the people and groups that they interact with. This is not to say that people cannot think or believe differently. It is simply an assertion that behavioral norms exist and that they are the boundaries within which we create understanding between others and ourselves.

Without behavioral norms to guide our collective interactions with each other, our actions and words may create an incorrect understanding of our intentions.

What do you think?

What are some behavioral norms that are particularly important to you? Why?

_____

_____

_____

---

[7] Public Papers of the Presidents of the United States (1987 edition)

Behavioral Awareness

After we have identified the behavioral norms that we deem important for pursuing life, liberty, and happiness, the next step in CBIP is behavioral awareness. Although our behavior is observable and in plain view for everyone to see and interpret, some people may not be aware of their own behavior in relation to the behavioral norms.

To become behaviorally aware, one must become conscious of oneself within contexts involving others.

Behavioral awareness happens when conscious decision-making starts and acting on impulse (without thinking) stops. When we consciously consider (think about) something and then make a choice among different behavioral alternatives, we become aware of and therefore responsible for our behavioral actions. In addition, it is infinitely wiser to think about what we do before we do it.

The development of the capacity to think before acting is what differentiates adulthood from adolescence and, for that matter, distinguishes humans from all other life forms on the planet. Legally, *adulthood* starts at the age of eighteen years. At eighteen, we are legally responsible for our behavioral decision-making.

Individuals who are over the age of eighteen years and repeatedly demonstrate patterns of impulsive conduct are not behaviorally aware, and are therefore adolescents disguised as adults. Without behavioral awareness we cannot fully understand the impact of our decision-making on others or on the trajectory of our lives. Without behavioral awareness we cannot accurately identify our own behavioral strengths, weaknesses, and behavioral tendencies.

What do you think?

Are you your thoughts, or are you the thinker of your thoughts? Which statement do you agree with more? Why?

_____

_____

_____

_____

Behavioral Strengths and Weaknesses

After a person becomes behaviorally aware, he or she is capable of objectively and accurately identifying his or her own behavioral strengths and weaknesses. That does not mean that he or she will do so; it just means that he or she has become conscious of his or her own behavior. Whether an individual develops a sophisticated understanding of one's behavior is a function of his or her *willingness* to objectively examine his or her own thoughts, feelings, and actions. This is called relection.

In his seminal article entitled, "Managing Oneself," Peter Drucker, wrote that, "success in the knowledge economy comes to those who know themselves – their strengths, their values, and how they perform best."[8] Drucker believed that one of the most important things people should figure out about themselves is what they do best so that they can make their *greatest contribution*. In his view, people can perform best only from strength, but they must be aware of their own *unproductive habits* (weaknesses) that prevent them from achieving the outcomes that they desire.

Only after a person understands his or her unique combination of behavioral strengths and weaknesses can she or he create an informed long-term plan for behavioral success. Although identifying information about yourself is a lifelong process, you will begin the process of defining your own *behavioral* strengths and weaknesses throughout this book. By understanding behavioral norms, developing behavioral awareness, and clarifying your behavioral strengths and weaknesses, you will be in a better position to create informed and meaningful behavioral goals for yourself.

What do you think?

Have you done as well as you could have in school or at work? If not, what could you have done that could have helped you be more successful? Please list three things that you would like to improve about yourself.

_____

_____

_____

_____

---

[8] Drucker, Peter F., "Managing Oneself", Harvard Business Review, On Point Article, Product 4444, Jan. 2005, page 1

Behavioral Goal

A goal is an end state that one strives to attain. There are many types of goals including professional, personal, spiritual, financial, and behavioral. Behavioral goals are …

the values and character traits that a person aspires to display.

Why is it important to figure out the type of person that you aspire to be and what you want to stand for? Your behavioral choices transmit information about your values, ethics, judgment, manner, emotions, friendliness, interest, desire, motivation, attitude, aptitude, dependability, and work ethic. In short …

our behavioral choices reveal our values and character.

How other people perceive us, and how we perceive ourselves, is largely a consequence of our own behavioral decision-making. Like a compass, behavioral goals point us in the right direction when we make choices. But unlike a compass that only points us in a particular direction, behavioral goals help us deal with all of the difficult obstacles and struggles that we encounter along our journey. All journeys end at destinations. Behavioral goals are destinations. Without behavioral goals, how would we know if our choices were moving us in the right direction?

What do you think?

What character traits (social, emotional, physical, and intellectual) do you want people to think of when they think of you? Please make a list of one-word adjectives that you would like other people to use to described you.

1. _____

2. _____

3. _____

4. _____

5. _____

Behavioral Evaluation

Our choices about what we say and do, how reliable we are, how hard we work, how nice we are to others, how we communicate, are all in plain view for others to see. As such, our behavior provides information about our nature and character that can be collected, measured, and evaluated to help people understand each other.

*Our behavior demonstrates our values
and our willingness to adhere to behavioral norms.*

Our behavior in school, work, relationships, and in everyday life reveals traits to the world traits about our maturity level, nature, and character (good and bad). It also shows others that we know how to successfully navigate (or not) the world. To see how one might objectively evaluate behavior, consider the following scenario.

Think about it

Three brothers are sitting on a couch after dinner, and there is a big pile of dishes sitting in the sink waiting to be washed. One of the brothers is responsible, one is somewhat responsible, and one is irresponsible. How can you tell which brother is which?

_____

_____

Answer

The responsible brother gets up and *willingly* does the dishes *without* needing to be asked. The somewhat responsible brother does the dishes, but only after being asked. The irresponsible brother doesn't do the dishes, even after being asked.[9]

Our behavior demonstrates the degree to which we have developed the ability to regulate ourselves. Individuals who need to be asked or told to do basic things such as caring for others,

---

[9] As stated in the South Eastern Kentucky Community College presentation at the 2015 National Institute for Staff and Organizational Development (NISOD) Conference in Austin TX.

exhibiting commitment, making good choices, or communicating appropriately demonstrate that these basic behavioral traits are not yet woven through the fabric of who they are. They demonstrate that they have either not yet developed the ability to self-regulate or are unwilling to do so. Either way, the experience of dealing with people who require behavioral guidance (or adult supervision) is completely different from interacting with people who do not require behavioral guidance. People who need to be told to be nice or show up or work hard are very different from people who don't need to be told to do these basic things.

The key to understanding and evaluating behavior in ourselves and others is the degree to which we *willingly* do that which is our own responsibility and we accept that our behavior is our most important responsibility.

Responsible people are accountable for their own behavior.

Responsible people self-manage. They have a palpable sense of duty about their obligations (to themselves and others). Conversely, people who do not *willingly* act in a responsible manner require behavioral guidance; they cannot be confidently relied on to fulfill their obligations unless others supervise them. Even with supervision, some people don't fulfill their obligations.

There is an inverse relationship between trust and guidance; the more behavioral guidance required to fulfill our basic behavioral obligations, the less we can be entrusted with responsibility (Figure 3). Students who need to be told to do their homework or to go to class require behavioral guidance. The experience of dealing with students that need to be told what to do behaviorally is completely different from dealing with students who don't need to be told to do these things.

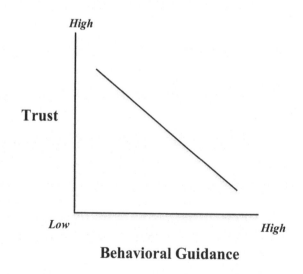

(Figure 3)

The opposite is also true of course: The less behavioral guidance people require, the more they demonstrate that they can be entrusted with responsibility.

> ***Behavior that requires guidance from others is by definition
> not self-managed behavior.***

Self-management skills are particularly important for students because they are *self-employed*. Students work for themselves. As such, they are their own bosses. While it is a self-evident truth that students who choose to work hard by putting in long hours of studying, attending all of their classes, rewriting their class notes, completing all of their assignments, and attending tutoring sessions understand their academic subject matter much better and outperform students who do not do these things. However, many other students still do not work hard.

Many students have a tough time making the connection between their own behavioral performance and their academic performance. If they don't do well in school, they may even mistakenly assume that they are not *academically inclined*, when in fact, they may never have behaved in a manner consistent with doing well in school. They may never have taken the time required (by everyone) to actually learn the material. They may never have behaved like students.

Think about it

Three sisters (triplets) recently graduated from high school together, and they live at home with their parents in upstate, NY. All three sisters are enrolled at a community college. They all have identical schedules and have enrolled in the following courses:

Self-Management	3 credit
College Writing	3 credits
Chemistry 1 with Lab	4 credits
Microeconomics	3 credits
College Algebra and Trigonometry	<u>3 credits</u>
	16 credits

They arrive home after the first day of the semester and have a lot of homework. One of the sisters is committed to college, one is not committed to college, and one is somewhere in between. How could you tell which is which?

Self-Management:
Understanding, Communicating and Assessing
Behavioral Competency, 3rd Edition
Gian Paolo Roma - © 2019 - All Rights Reserved

Answer:

The sister who independently (without guidance from others) follows through and does all of her work, including going to class, without having to be asked to do so is the most committed to college. This sister communicates that she can be entrusted with the responsibility of going to college because she willingly manages her own affairs. This sister does not require guidance to be successful.

The sister who needs to be asked or told to do her schoolwork and go to class, but eventually does so, is somewhat committed to college. Although this sister fulfills her obligations, she is unwilling to manage her responsibilities without guidance from others. This sister requires guidance from other to be successful.

The sister that fails to follow through and meet her obligations, even with guidance from others, communicates that she cannot be entrusted with the responsibilities of college.

Evaluating Behavior [10]

Because each of the 5Cs is defined in terms of specific behavioral standards, they accurately describe what reflects more or less effective behavioral performance. The 5Cs are core behavioral standards that can apply to everyone, regardless of societal rank or station in life, not just to students or children. They provide the lens through which behavior can be objectively viewed and evaluated.

The major advantages of defining each of the behavioral competencies in this manner are:

1. To help people set their own expectations of themselves;
2. To help people decide for themselves what they should expect from others; and
3. To provide a common standard to evaluate the experience of interacting with others, thereby improving consistency, situational judgment, and decision-making. Below is the 5C self-management behavioral observation performance model.[11]

Below Expectations	Meets Expectations	Role Model
Even with guidance, fails to provide evidence *(verbal, written, and behavioral)* that they communicate appropriately, prioritize important matters ahead of unimportant matters, show thoughtful concern for others, follow through and meet obligations, and adapt effectively to difficult, changing, and complex circumstances.	With guidance, provides evidence *(verbal, written, and behavioral)* that they communicate appropriately, prioritize important matters ahead of unimportant matters, show thoughtful concern for others, follow through and meet obligations, and adapt effectively to difficult, changing, and complex circumstances.	Independently provides evidence *(verbal, written, and behavioral)* that they communicate appropriately, prioritize important matters ahead of unimportant matters, show thoughtful concern for others, follow through and meet obligations, and adapt effectively to difficult, changing, and complex circumstances.
Even with guidance, fails to provide evidence of these behaviors and is unwilling to work on the responsibility of self-management.	With guidance, provides evidence of these behaviors and is willing to work on being responsible.	Willingly provides evidence of these behaviors and can be trusted with responsibility.

The three performance standards set forth three different behavioral effectiveness levels (Below Expectations, Meets Expectations, and Role Model).[12] Each of these levels will be discussed in more detail in later units.

---

[10] Adapted from SHRM Effective Practice Guideline by Pulakos, Elaine D., (2004) entitled "Performance Management - A Roadmap for Developing, Implementing and Evaluating Performance Management Systems" p. 10-14, Society of Human Resources Management (SHRM) Foundation.

[11] Ibid, Pulakos (2004), p. 10.

Notice that the key differentiating factors between the different effectiveness levels are *willingness*, and the degree to which we require *behavioral guidance*. The more independently willingly a person demonstrates the 5Cs without guidance, the more effective he or she is at managing his or her own behavior. The Role Model level willingly behaves as expected. The Meets Expectation level does what is expected but not without behavioral guidance. And the Below Expectation level does not do what is expected even with guidance.

It is important to remember that a person can be deemed a "Role Model" at one competency, but be Below Expectations at another. For example, a person might be evaluated as being a Role Model at commitment to school, but be Below Expectation when it comes to being caring to other students or faculty. The behaviorally competent individual is aware of and working on all of the 5Cs, not just one or two.

The three different performance levels (Below Expectations, Meets Expectations, and Role Model) can be further broken down into a five-point Behavioral Observation Scale (BOS). The BOS measures how consistently a person demonstrates or models the 5C behaviors. [13]

---

5 = Almost always performs as described by the Role Model standard.

4 = Sometimes performs as described by the Role Model standard and sometimes performs as described by the Meets Expectations standards.

3 = Almost always performs as described by the Meets Expectations standard.

2 = Sometimes performs as described by the Meets Expectations standard and sometimes performs as described by the Below Expectations standards.

1 = Almost always performs as described by the Below Expectations standard.

What do you think?

For each statement, and using the Behavioral Observation Scale described above, write in the right-hand margin the number (1, 2, 3, 4 or 5) corresponding to the degree to which you consistently exhibit the behavior described in the statement. Note that there are no right or wrong answers. All that is important is that you indicate how consistently you exhibit the behavior described in the action statement.

---

[12] Ibid, Pulakos (2004), p.10.
[13] Op. Cit., Pulakos (2004), p.14

	Trust Category	Rating (1-5)
Communication	I communicate appropriately.	
Choice	I prioritize important matters ahead of unimportant matters when I make decisions.	
Commitment	I follow through and meet obligations.	
Coping	I adapt effectively to difficult, changing, and complex circumstances.	
Caring	I show thoughtful concern for others.	
AVERAGE		

This quick assessment shows how the Behavioral Observation Scale works and how the 5Cs relate to you. How did you rank your overall behavioral effectiveness? What was your average? Explain your answer.

_____

_____

_____

_____

Behavioral Observation Scales and your individual assessments results for each of the 5Cs are used throughout this book and will be logged into the Employability Profile on the next page and at the end of each unit. Once logged, a simple arithmetic mean or average can be used to calculate a Behavioral Competency Rating. An additional copy of the Employability Profile can be found in Appendix I at the back of the book. The Appendix I copy should be kept blank in case additional copies are needed.

Tracking your behavioral performance in this way will help you compare and assess your actual behavior against your own defined behavioral standards and against the 5C standards established in this book. This comparison will help you understand the extent to which your performance deviates from what you expect from yourself, and from what others expect from you. After you understand how your behavior deviates from the standards you set for yourself, you can take the necessary actions to improve your performance. However, it is important to keep in mind that some minor deviations in performance can be expected. You are not a machine. So, try concentrating your attention on big deviations in your behavioral performance instead of trying to control each and every deviation.

Recommended for Employment [Select]	Total Work-Based Learning Hours [Select]	Portfolio Completed [Select]	Passed State/National Assessment [Select]
1	2	3	4	5

Below Expectations

Even with guidance, fails to provide evidence *(verbal, written, and behavioral)* that they communicate appropriately, prioritize important matters ahead of unimportant matters, show thoughtful concern for others, follow through and meet obligations, and adapt effectively to difficult, changing, and complex circumstances.

Even with guidance, fails to provide evidence of these behaviors and is unwilling to work on trust and responsibility.

Meets Expectations

With guidance, provides evidence *(verbal, written, and behavioral)* that they communicate appropriately, prioritize important matters ahead of unimportant matters, show thoughtful concern for others, follow through and meet obligations, and adapt effectively to difficult, changing, and complex circumstances.

With guidance, provides evidence of these behaviors and is willing to work on trust responsibility.

Role Model

Independently provides evidence *(verbal, written, and behavioral)* that they communicate appropriately, prioritize important matters ahead of unimportant matters, show thoughtful concern for others, follow through and meet obligations, and adapt effectively to difficult, changing, and complex circumstances.

Willingly provides evidence of these behaviors and can be trusted with responsibility.

Where:

5 = Almost always performs as described by the "Role Model" standard.

4 = Sometimes performs as described by the 'Role Model" standard and sometimes performs as described by the "Meets Expectations" standard.

3 = Almost always performs as described by the "Meets Expectations" standard.

2 = Sometimes performs as described by the "Meets Expectations' standard and sometimes performs as described by the "Below Expectations' standard.

1 = Almost always performs as described by the "Below Expectations' standard.

Communication
Trust a person to convey messages appropriately to others.

	Audience
	Involvement
	Message
	Evidence
	COMMUNICATION MEAN

Choices
Trust a person to prioritize important matters ahead of unimportant matters.

	Communication
	Commitment
	Coping
	Caring
	CHOICE MEAN

BEHAVIORAL COMPETENCY RATING (BCR) (MEAN OF MEANS)

Commitment
Trust a person to follow through and meet obligations.

	Dependability	Attendance
	Dependability	Accountability
	Dependability	Contribution
	Hard Work	Time / Deliberate Practice
	Hard Work	Delayed Gratification
	Hard Work	Effort / Energy
	Hard Work	Effort / Determination
	Hard Work	Effort / Stamina
	Quality	Measure of Excellence
	Quality	Continuous Improvement
	COMMITMENT MEAN	

Coping
Trust a person to handle and adapt effectively to difficult, changing, and complex circumstances

	Coping	Change / Demonstration
	Coping	Adversity / Self-Awareness
	Coping	Adversity / Self-Restraint
	Coping	Adversity / Self-Improvement
	Coping	Complexity / Capability
	Coping	Complexity / Capacity
	COPING MEAN	

Caring
Trust a person to show thoughtful concern for others.

	Caring	Consideration / Listening
	Caring	Consideration / Courtesy
	Caring	Consideration / Respectful
	Caring	Concern / Cooperation
	Caring	Concern / Helpful
	Caring	Concern / Compromise
	Caring	Conscientious / Thoughtful
	Caring	Conscientious / Careful
	Caring	Conscientious / Fair
	CARING MEAN	

Behavioral Adjustment

"When you know how to create tiny habits, you can change your life forever."[14]

~ BJ Fogg

Knowing what we should do and *doing* what we should do are two different things. We *know* what we should be doing; the hard part is actually *doing* what we should be doing. We have a "knowing/doing" gap in our society. For instance, all students know that they should go to class and study. For 13 years before college from K-12, teachers drill into their students the importance of showing up to class on time and doing homework. Yet, each year hundreds of thousands of students are academically dismissed from colleges because they miss class and/or do not do their homework.

If you have struggled with doing what you are supposed to do, you may want to consider the work of Stanford University researcher Dr. BJ Fogg that focuses on changing behaviors in positive ways.[15] According to Dr. Fogg's Behavior Model (FBM) (Figure 4), three variables must converge at the same moment for any behavior to occur: motivation, ability, and trigger. If any of these three variables change, it's not the same behavior.

Fogg's Behavior Model (FBM)[16]

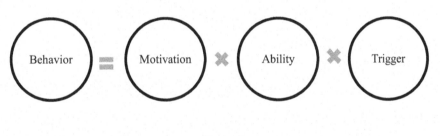

Figure 4

When a behavior does not occur (such as studying, doing homework, or going to class), at least one of these three elements is missing. Either the person is not motivated to perform the desired behavior, doesn't have the ability to perform the desired behavior, or doesn't have a prompt that reminds the person to do the desired behavior.

---

[14] Fogg, BJ, (2014, December). Tiny surprises for happiness and health. Retrieved from
https://www.youtube.com/watch?v=2L1R7OtJhWs

[15] Fogg, BJ, Stanford University, http://www.tinyhabits.com

[16] Adapted from Fogg, BJ model described at www.behaviormodel.org

For instance, if a student is continually late to class, he or she is either not motivated to get to class, doesn't have the ability to get to class, or doesn't have a trigger that reminds him or her to go to class. If a student is motivated and has the ability to get to class (we can call this will and skill), then the trigger may be to set an alarm 1 hour before class to trigger the thought to get to class. Although this seems simple enough, many students don't have triggers to remind them about things that they need to do. If triggers are set and an individual still does not do the desired behavior, then the cause of the behavioral issue is either motivation (will) or ability (skill).

According to FBM, we will do a desired behavior when our motivation and ability are above the action line, (Figure 5) and we get a trigger to do the behavior. Looking at Figure 5, if we make the desired behavior too hard, we will not do it.

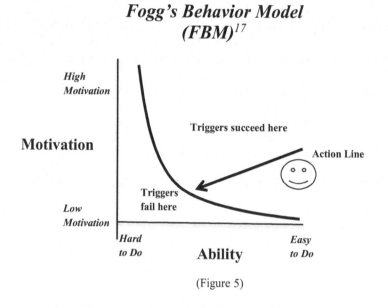

(Figure 5)

The key to FBM is to create new tiny habits that are easy to do and require little motivation, and to also figure out a trigger to activate the new tiny habit. Doing things that are hard to do requires a lot of motivation.

How do we trigger the new tiny habits? According to Dr. Fogg, rather than trying to change our existing behaviors, "we make our existing behavior the event that triggers the desired behavior." For example, suppose that you want to start exercising more, you might use your existing morning routine to trigger a new tiny habit exercise routine. Let's say that you make coffee in the morning; you could make the habit of making coffee the trigger that initiates a new tiny habit exercise routine

---

[17] Op. Cit., BJ Fogg FBM Model

like walking up and down a flight of the stairs in your house *once*. On the second day you could walk up and down the steps twice, and so on until you can walk up and down the steps for the entire time the coffee is brewing. If a coffee pot takes five minutes to brew, you might be able to walk up and down the steps 20 times within a few weeks. If we make the exercise routine too strenuous and difficult on the first day, we may not want to continue because big behavior changes require too much internal motivation (coaxing) to do. According to Dr. Fogg, "if we keep repeating the tiny habits, over time they will become the new habit because of repetition."

Habits are about repeating behaviors.

We will be using the tiny habits technique at the end of each unit to help coax and nurture the behaviors covered in this course.

Changing Habits

How do you employ tiny habits in your life? As you think about changing your habits, think about framing the tiny habit in the following format suggested by Dr. Fogg:

Format for a tiny habit:

> *After I <u>(insert existing behavior)</u>,*
>
> *I will <u>(insert new tiny behavior)</u>.*

Example:

"After I am awakened by my alarm, I will put one foot on the ground."

Please take a few moments and try to come up with one tiny habit that you can use to help you improve your behavioral performance. Remember to use the, "After I <u>(insert existing behavior)</u>, I will <u>(insert new tiny behavior)</u>."

After I _____,

I will _____.

Personal Policy Contract

One of the greatest challenges you will have in college and life is managing your own behavior. As stated earlier, you probably *know* what you should be doing; the hard part is actually *doing* what you should be doing. If you really want to change your own behavior and achieve your goals, whatever they may be, research shows that people who write down specific goals are far more likely to be successful than those who do not write down their goals or have no goals at all.[18]

To help you achieve your behavioral goals, you will be writing them down and creating Personal Policy Contracts like the one below. By signing and dating the Personal Policy Contract, it becomes an obligation to yourself that cannot be broken.

Behavioral Goal: _____

Goals	Example: I will work on the following behavioral goals in college. [Types of goals may include: improve my dependability, completing homework, studying better, improving work ethic, appropriateness, reducing school stress, improving time management and judgment]
Personal Policies	Example: Personal policies I commit to so that I can achieve my goal. [Types personal policies may include I will never miss class or be late to class, I will study at least two hours every day, I will stop and think about my audience before communicate, I will actively listen, never miss an assignment, I will ask questions in class if I don't understand the academic material]
Public Commitments	Example: Public commitments that I will make to regularly measure how I am doing relative to my goals and personal policies. I will send my goals, personal policies, and quick weekly progress reports to a supportive friend and the professor. [Types of progress reports include, "I didn't miss any classes this week", or "I studied three hours on Monday, four hours, Tuesday, I turned my phone off before every class]

Signature: _____ *Date:* _____

---

[18] Matthews, Gail, Dominican University, https://www.dominican.edu/academics/lae/undergraduate-programs/psych/faculty/assets-gail-matthews/researchsummary2.pdf

Important Terms

The following terms will help you, particularly if you learn how to explain them and use them in the right places and situations.

Self-Management
Trust
Behavioral Competency
5Cs of Self-Management
Trust Dimension
Behavioral Occurrence
Behavioral Pattern
Continuous Behavioral Improvement Process
Willingness

Behavioral Guidance
Behavioral Norms
Behavioral Awareness
Behavioral Strengths and Weaknesses
Behavioral Goal
Behavioral Evaluation
Behavioral Observations Scale (BOS)
Fogg's Behavioral Model (FBM)
Tiny Habits

Discussion of Meanings

1. What is the basic idea of self-management?
2. Have you ever found yourself in an embarrassing situation because you didn't act in a trustworthy manner? Explain what you did not do that was not trustworthy.
3. What is the difference between a trust definition and a trust dimension?
4. What is a behavioral occurrence? What is a behavioral pattern? Describe an example of each.
5. "It doesn't matter who I'm talking to, I am always the same." Discuss this statement. Do you agree with it?
6. What are the advantages of acting in a behaviorally competent manner? What are the disadvantages? Overall, do you think that behaving in a behaviorally competent manner is a good idea?
7. Explain the terms "skill" and "will" as they relate to behavioral evaluation.
8. What does the author mean when he says that trust is multifaceted?
9. What is the difference between a "role model" and a "meets expectation" behavioral rating?
10. Why are behavioral norms so important?
11. What was the main point of the "3 brothers on a couch" exercise?
12. Explain Fogg's Behavioral Model (FBM).
13. The Behavioral Observation Scale has 5-levels. Describe each level.
14. There are 3 behavioral effectiveness performance standards (role model, meets expectations, and below expectations). Explain the different levels and give examples to illustrate your points.
15. According to FBM, when will a person make sure that he or she does a desired behavior?

Practice True/False Self-Test
(Explain if false)

Is each of the following statements *True* or *False*? Circle the best answer. If your answer is false, briefly describe why. (Hint: All of the answers are false)

For example:

1. The trust definition for Consideration is "Trust a person to show a thoughtful concern for others."   True or *False*

    The answer is false because "Trust a person to show thoughtful concern for others" is the trust definition for Caring not Consideration.

---

1. Trust is defined as having a palpable sense of duty about one's obligations towards others.   True or False

2. The three variables in Fogg's Behavior Model are skill, will, and energy.   True or False

3. The continuous behavioral improvement process starts with behavioral awareness.   True or False

4. A behavioral pattern is a one-time event or single behavioral incident that happens.   True or False

5. There is a parallel relationship between trust and behavioral guidance.

True or False

6. Behavioral competency is defined as the ability to achieve one's goals in a trustworthy manner.

True or False

7. The five variables in the 5C model are character, courage, capability, courtesy, and cooperation.

True or False

8. Behavioral Goals are social qualities or characteristics that are deemed essential for living together in society.

True or False

9. The 5-point performance measurement scale described in this unit is known as a Likert Scale.

True or False

10. According to FBM, a person will do a desired behavior when the person's skill and will are below the action line.

True or False

To Sum Up

How other people perceive us, and how we perceive ourselves, is largely a consequence of our own behavioral decision-making. In life, we are making choices every moment of every day. Like a compass, behavioral goals point us in the right direction when we are considering various behavioral alternatives and making behavioral choices. But unlike a compass that only points you in a particular direction, behavioral goals help us deal with all of the difficult obstacles we will encounter on our journeys. Without behavioral goals, how would we know if we were going in the right direction?

Although academic ability is important, it does not guarantee academic success.

Each year, millions of smart students drop out of college because they are unable to manage their own behavior.

Because certain behaviors lead to better performance than others, it is appropriate and necessary for you to study, understand, and evaluate the relationship between your behavior and your performance.

Johann Wolfgang Von Goethe wrote more than 200 years ago, "Behavior is the mirror in which everyone shows their image." Your behavior communicates a great deal about you. Your academic performance (good or bad) will be largely the result of your behavior. Because you are responsible for how you communicate, how you make choices, how considerate you are of others, how committed you are to the activities you are involved with, and how well you cope with difficulty in your life, it is appropriate and necessary for you to study and understand the relationship between your behavior and your performance.

Use this book to help you develop your own strategies for improving your behavioral performance. Understanding and controlling your own behavior will affect not only your academic future but also your life after graduation.

Unit 2

Communication

Self-Management:
Understanding, Communicating and Assessing
Behavioral Competency, 3rd Edition
Gian Paolo Roma - © 2019 - All Rights Reserved

Understanding Communication

"The most important thing in communication is hearing what isn't said."

~ Peter F. Drucker

In 1967, three communication theorists named Watzlawick, Bevin, and Jackson coined the axiom: "One cannot *not* communicate."[19] Everything we do communicates some kind of message about us. "Activity or inactivity, words or silence all have message value: they influence others and these others, in turn, cannot not respond to these communications and are thus themselves communicating."[20] So, everything we say and do communicates facts and information about ourselves that influence how others see us. Our actions and words profoundly affect others' beliefs about and behavior towards us. What and how we communicate helps others determine our underlying nature and whether or not they want to associate with us. It is through our own communications that people figure us out. People decide to like us, trust us, hire us, or even to marry us based on what and how we communicate.

Interestingly, most of what people communicate every moment of every day has very little to do with words. Research shows that only about seven percent of communication involves words.[21] When you think about it, it is astounding that humans are the only life form on the planet that use words to communicate. Words help humans explain and understand the context and meaning of the world, but they are only a small part of how people communicate.

A simple thought experiment illustrates how this works. The feelings and emotions associated with love are the same around the world, but love has a different name in each language. In Czech, it's láska; in Russian; любовь; and in Turkish, aşk. The word for love is not the feeling or emotion of being in love. If two people don't speak the same language, would they still be able to communicate a deep affection for one another? Feelings, moods, emotions, and actions all speak for themselves. They communicate a great deal without words.

In fact, research shows that more than 93% of communication does not involve words.[22] We communicate with our voice inflection and our nonverbal communications, such as our body language and actions. What we do and how we behave conveys messages to others about our feelings and the kind of people we are. Importantly, we are not credible when our words are not

---

[19] Watzlawick, P., Beavin, J., and Jackson, D., (1967). Pragmatics of Human Communication. W. W. Norton: New York. p1.

[20] Ibid, Watzlawick, Beavin, and Jackson (1967)p1.

[21] Mehrabian, A. and Wiener, M. (1967). Decoding of Inconsistent Communications, *Journal of Personality and Social Psychology,* 6, 109-114.

[22] Ibid, Mehrabian and Wiener (1967).

backed up by our actions. To that extent, our actions and deeds are what are real about us and therefore define who we are to others. They convey information about our true nature, as opposed to our words which only explain how we might like to be seen. We continually send information nonverbally about our values, ethics, judgment, manner, emotions, friendliness, interest, desire, motivation, attitude, aptitude, dependability, and work ethic. Although writing and speaking skills are important, nonverbal communication reveals a great deal more about our true nature. We can define communication as …

the process that creates understanding between people.

As the definition implies, communication is not a one-way street. To create understanding between people, one must have a predisposition to listen and authentically appreciate the ideas, feelings, and thoughts of others. Inherent in this definition is the recognition of the value and significance of other people and things. People that communicate effectively value others.

Because "one cannot not communicate,"[23] one is either effective or ineffective at creating understanding between people, or somewhere in between. Effective communication produces desired or intended results, while ineffective communication can create an incorrect understanding of our intentions, which can lead to the opposite result. Although willingness to cooperate is affected by many factors other than the messages that you communicate, (for example, organizational culture, workload, past experience) what and how you communicate should *not* be a barrier to what you seek. As such, effective communication will be fundamental to your success in college and throughout life.

The focus of this unit is to improve the effectiveness of *your* communication. Its purpose is to aid you in communicating in a way that supports you in achieving your goals. Specifically, we want to try to determine what messages are important to people and ensure that your communications satisfy those requirements. To communicate more effectively you will learn how to A.I.M.E. when you communicate.

Audience	The people with whom you communicate.
Involvement	The connection (strong/weak) that you have with each audience type.
Message	The substance and meaning of a communication.
Evidence	Plainly visible criteria that audiences will use in forming conclusions or judgments about you.

---

[23] Op. sit., Watzlawick, Beavin, & Jackson, (1967).

Audience

The first step in communicating effectively is to identify the different people with whom you interact and define the characteristics that are unique to each group. We will call the different types of people that we interact with audience types. Gathering detailed information on the characteristics of audience types will put you in a better position to gauge the appropriateness of the messages that you communicate when you interact with others.

Think About It

Before we go any further, take a few minutes to jot down some of the different audience types with whom you interact regularly. Try to make the list as comprehensive as possible.

Audience Types:

1. _____   4. _____

2 _____   5. _____

3. _____   6. _____

Involvement

Now that you have identified the different audience types, let's define how you are involved with each type. For example, it is not enough to say, "I am my parent's child." What does it feel like from the perspective of a parent, or professor, or employer? What are the drives, goals, and opinions of the different audience types regarding their involvement with you? Involvement looks at whether or not an audience type cares much about the outcomes of your behavioral choices. Some audience types will care a great deal about you and your behavior, and some will not. In general, …

audience types with a big stake in your behavior (i.e., those whose success and or reason for being relies on your behavior) will have high degrees of concern about your behavior.

The opposite is also true. Audience types that are not impacted much by your behavior will have lower degrees of concern about your behavior.

Self-Management:
Understanding, Communicating and Assessing
Behavioral Competency, 3rd Edition
Gian Paolo Roma - © 2019 - All Rights Reserved

Think About It

You will have varying levels of involvement with many audiences. Regardless of whom you are communicating with, understanding what motivates and is important to each audience type will help you judge the appropriateness of your messages. How involved are you with the audience types that you identified above?

(In other words, how are the audiences impacted by your behavior?)

	Audience	Involvement Level (Low, Medium, High)	Involvement (Describe your audience involvement)
1			
2			
3			
4			
5			
6			

Message

When you interact with others, it is important to remember that talking and writing are not the main ways you communicate. As we discussed earlier, only seven percent of the substance and meaning of what you communicate is conveyed using words.[24] Yet many people try to explain their own behavior using words. This can be problematic because communicating with words through writing and speaking is actually quite difficult to do well. To give you an idea of how difficult it is to communicate effectively using words, imagine trying to describe with words the two drawings below. Imagine trying to write down the description of the two shapes and how they are positioned in the drawing. How many words would you need to clearly describe what you are seeing?

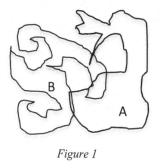

Figure 1

Although difficult to describe with words, the image is easy to understand. The image visually communicates. In the same way that the image speaks for itself, so too does your behavior. Your behavior reveals your true feelings, moods, emotions, intentions, nature, and character. And because behavior speaks for itself, words that contradict behavior (do not walk the talk) reveal integrity-related issues, which affect character. In fact ….

integrity is revealed when our words and behaviors are in alignment.

Remember, everything that you do has message value. By making sure that your words and actions are in alignment, you will be in a better position to communicate with integrity … a fundamental building block of trust. Trust is the single most important message that you can communicate to the various audience types that are highly involved with you. Long-term healthy relations with others are built upon foundations of trust. Stephen Covey writes that, "Trust is the glue of life. It's

---

[24] Op. Cit., Mehrabian and Wiener, (1967) p. 28.

the most essential ingredient in effective communication. It's the foundational principle that holds all relationships."[25] If people trust you, they will be more willing to associate with and help you.

What do you think?

The messages below are actual e-mails from students to professors. What messages are the students communicating about themselves in these messages? Please use one word statements to describe the messages the students are sending about themselves to their professors.

	Message (s)
"heyyyy, i know i havent been there for a while but things have just bee crazy i went to va then go sick but il be back thur can you give me any work is missed/??"	
"hey i was wondering if you could send me the homework and everything else that we did in class and again i am sorry that i could not be there but if you would send me the homework for monday and last monday and wednesday please so that i can get what we did in class and so i can study the things and know what we did thank you that would be great thankyou see you on monday and sorry that i could not e there"	
"I know u have been absent and made you upset . I know when u looked at me you saw potential this going away college was just difficult for me I just hope you have in your heart to pass me I probably did let you down and you didn't want see that from me because I had you before I was trying pass all my other classes just so I won't be kicked out of school you may say I'm begging and I am you might say it won't be fare for others but I always at your class just late and just didn't sign in those 6 times I saw the videos u put up I was there when u helped people with the schedule I couldn't do my schedule because I owe the school money and they had me on hold"	
"eye will find out, eye'm gonna have to call the library. 9-noon, thats three hours That is enough time for me to take both, right? Yeah i'm good with that."	

Remember, "One cannot not communicate." You are always communicating. In the same way that these students revealed what is true about themselves in their e-mails and their behavior toward their professors, your actions and words reveal what is real and true about you. Do your actions and words communicate that you are responsible and trustworthy?

---

[25] Covey, Stephen R. *The 7 Habits of Highly Effective People: Restoring the Character Ethic.* (Rev. ed.). New York: Free Press, 2004.

Evidence

People sift through your communications looking for behavioral evidence that you are trustworthy in all five of the trust categories. They want to see that you make good decisions regarding the people in your life, activities you are involved with, and situations that you encounter. Do you handle all of them well, or do you sometimes fall short in some way? People who do *all* of these things consistently well can be given responsibility because they have proven that they can be trusted to handle people, activities, and situations effectively. Although it is difficult to do all of these things well simultaneously, it is what behaviorally competent individuals strive to do.

How can you assess behavioral trustworthiness in people? Although it is difficult to gauge trustworthiness, there are ways. One way is to look for evidence of behavioral patterns. People with patterns of behavior often leave behind clues about the way they behave.

For example, for an individual to be deemed to be considerate of others, there must be an absence of inconsiderate behavior towards others. Patterns of belittling, demeaning, or undermining others regularly would be evidence of inconsiderate behavior. If there are patterns of evidence that a person behaves in this way towards others, then the evidence would suggest that the individual is not considerate.

Another example, for an individual to be deemed capable of coping with difficult, changing, or complex situations, there should be an absence of patterns of failing to cope with these types of situations. If evidence of patterns of failure to cope emerge, then it is reasonable to infer that the individual may not cope well with similar challenging situations in the future.

Similarly, for an individual to be deemed to be committed to an activity, there should be an absence of patterns of uncommitted behavior. If the evidence indicates patterns of uncommitted behavior to an activity, then it is reasonable to assume that the individual has other priorities and is not as committed to that activity. This is not to say that behavior cannot change. However, it does suggest that unless one desires to change behavior, it will probably continue.

Remember, communicating effectively is not easy, and the consequences of sending conflicting messages can be severe. That is why it is important to be aware of whom you are communicating with (audience), the level of concern of each audience (involvement), and what you are communicating both verbally and non-verbally (message). When the evidence shows that your actions do not match your words, you erode trust because you send out contradictory messages.

To see if you are consistently sending messages that are in your best interest, please take a few minutes to complete the following self-assessment, *Communication Effectiveness: A Self-Assessment*, on the next page.

Communication Effectiveness: A Self-Assessment

Below Expectations	Meets Expectations	Role Model
Even with guidance, fails to demonstrate that **verbal, written, and behavioral** communications are appropriate and/or aligned with audience expectations. Even with guidance, fails to provide evidence of these behaviors and is unwilling to work on the responsibility of communicating appropriately.	With guidance, demonstrates that **verbal, written, and behavioral** communications are appropriate and aligned with audience expectations. With guidance, provides evidence of these behaviors and is willing to work on the responsibility of communicating appropriately.	Independently demonstrates that **verbal, written, and behavioral** communications are appropriate and aligned with audience expectations. Willingly provides evidence of these behaviors and can be trusted to communicate appropriately.

Using the Behavioral Observation Scale below as a guide, for each statement on the following page write in the rating column the number corresponding to the degree to which you consistently exhibit the behavior described in the statement. Note, there are no right or wrong answers. All that is important is that you indicate how consistently you exhibit the behavior described in the action statement.

Use the following Behavioral Observation Scale:

5 = Almost always performs as described by the Role Model standard.

4 = Sometimes performs as described by the Role Model standard and sometimes perform as described by the Meets Expectations standards.

3 = Almost always performs as described by the Meets Expectations standard.

2 = Sometimes performs as described by the Meets Expectations standard and sometimes perform as described by the Below Expectations standards.

1 = Almost always performs as described by the Below Expectations standard.

	Action Statement	Rating
1	I think about the best medium to communicate before I communicate (face to face, phone call, text message, voicemail, memo, e-mail, letter).	
2	I think about taking time to properly construct voice, text, and e-mail communications before I communicate out.	
3	I think about the most important messages that I am trying to communicate before I send out messages.	
4	I try to read the nonverbal cues of others and myself before I communicate.	
5	I think about my level of involvement with each audience when I communicate (High, Medium, or Low).	
6	I think about what's most important to me and the points of view of audiences when I communicate.	
7	I think about tailoring messages to ensure that the tone and content are appropriate to audiences when I communicate.	
8	I think about how my messages will impact my audience and myself when I communicate.	
9	I actively listen by asking questions and demonstrating attention to and conveying understanding of the comments and questions of others when I communicate.	
10	I control my emotions and remain positive even when demands are placed on me when I communicate.	
11	I make sure that my choice of actions and words communicate the same message when I communicate.	
12	I communicate clearly, using appropriate style, format, grammar, and tone when I communicate.	
13	I make sure that my choice of actions and words are respectful when I communicate (even when I'm upset).	
14	I make sure that my actions and words are timely when I communicate.	
15	I think about how my messages (choice of actions and words) will impact my character, relationships, and future when I communicate.	

Now transfer your answers for each statement into the corresponding space in the table below.

Communication Behavior: Mapping-Table

Item (n)	Behavior	A.I.M.E.	Behavior Rating	A.I.M.E. Average
1	Communication	Audience		
2	Communication	Audience		
3	Communication	Audience		
4	Communication	Involvement		
5	Communication	Involvement		
6	Communication	Involvement		
7	Communication	Involvement		
8	Communication	Message		
9	Communication	Message		
10	Communication	Message		
11	Communication	Message		
12	Communication	Message		
13	Communication	Message		
14	Communication	Message		
15	Communication	Evidence		
Average				

Average = ∑ of Behavior Rating/15:

Greater than 4: If your average is between 4 and 5, you are a good communicator, you avoid communication problems, and you require little guidance to communicate appropriately.

Between 3 and 4: If your average is greater than 3 but less than 4, with guidance you communicate appropriately, but occasionally you may be sending some messages that conflict with your goals.

Less than 3: If your average is less than 3, you sometimes communicate appropriately, but occasionally, even with guidance, you fail to communicate appropriately.

Take your A.I.M.E. averages for this section, calculate the new average of averages, and input that information into the Employability Profile on the following page.

Employability Profile — Student Name — Home School

Recommended for Employment [Select]	Total Work-Based Learning Hours [Select]	Portfolio Completed [Select]	Passed State/National Assessment [Select]
1	2	3	4	5

Below Expectations

Even with guidance, fails to provide evidence *(verbal, written, and behavioral)* that they communicate appropriately, prioritize important matters ahead of unimportant matters, show thoughtful concern for others, follow through and meet obligations, and adapt effectively to difficult, changing, and complex circumstances.

Even with guidance, fails to provide evidence of these behaviors and is unwilling to work on trust and responsibility.

Meets Expectations

With guidance, provides evidence *(verbal, written, and behavioral)* that they communicate appropriately, prioritize important matters ahead of unimportant matters, show thoughtful concern for others, follow through and meet obligations, and adapt effectively to difficult, changing, and complex circumstances.

With guidance, provides evidence of these behaviors and is willing to work on trust and responsibility.

Role Model

Independently provides evidence *(verbal, written, and behavioral)* that they communicate appropriately, prioritize important matters ahead of unimportant matters, show thoughtful concern for others, follow through and meet obligations, and adapt effectively to difficult, changing, and complex circumstances.

Willingly provides evidence of these behaviors and can be trusted with responsibility.

Where:

5 = Almost always performs as described by the "Role Model" standard.
4 = Sometimes performs as described by the "Role Model" standard and sometimes performs as described by the "Meets Expectations" standards.
3 = Almost always performs as described by the "Meets Expectations" standard.
2 = Sometimes performs as described by the "Meets Expectations" standard and sometimes performs as described by the "Below Expectations" standard.
1 = Almost always performs as described by the "Below Expectations" standard.

Communication
Trust a person to convey messages appropriately to others.

Audience	
Involvement	
Message	
Evidence	
COMMUNICATION MEAN	

Choices
Trust a person to prioritize important matters ahead of unimportant matters.

Communication	
Commitment	
Coping	
Caring	
CHOICE MEAN	

Commitment
Trust a person to follow through and meet obligations.

Dependability	Attendance
Dependability	Accountability
Dependability	Contribution
Hard Work	Time
Hard Work	Deliberate Practice
Hard Work	Delayed Gratification
Hard Work	Energy
Hard Work	Effort Determination
Hard Work	Effort Stamina
Quality	Measure of Excellence
Quality	Continuous Improvement
COMMITMENT MEAN	

Coping
Trust a person to handle and adapt effectively to difficult, changing, and complex circumstances

Coping	Change
Coping	Demonstration
Coping	Adversity Self-Awareness
Coping	Adversity Self-Restraint
Coping	Adversity Self-Improvement
Coping	Complexity Capability
Coping	Complexity Capacity
COPING MEAN	

Caring
Trust a person to show thoughtful concern for others.

Caring	Consideration Listening
Caring	Consideration Courtesy
Caring	Consideration Respectful
Caring	Concern Cooperation
Caring	Concern Helpful
Caring	Concern Compromise
Caring	Conscientious Thoughtful
Caring	Conscientious Careful
Caring	Conscientious Fair
CARING MEAN	

BEHAVIORAL COMPETENCY RATING (BCR) (MEAN OF MEANS)	

Think about It

In 1606 William Shakespeare wrote four centuries ago, "Mend your speech a little, lest you may mar your fortunes." As Shakespeare understood four centuries ago, communicating effectively is fundamental to human success. The Communication Behavior-Mapping Table shows you how appropriately you communicate to others. Do you communicate appropriately to others? If not, why not?

_____

_____

_____

_____

Changing Habits

How can you employ Fogg's Behavior Model tiny habits described earlier to improve how you communicate with people? As you think about changing your habits, think about framing the tiny habit in the following format suggested by Dr. Fogg:

Format for a tiny habit:

> **_After I (insert existing behavior),_**
>
> **_I will (insert new tiny behavior)._**

Please take a few moments and try to come up with one tiny communication habit that you can use to help you improve how you communicate. Remember to use the, "After I (insert existing behavior), I will (insert new tiny behavior)."

After I _____,

I will _____.

Important Terms

How well can you explain the following useful terms and phrases?

Communication
A.I.M.E.
Audience
Involvement
Message
Evidence
One Cannot Not Communicate

Conflicting or Contradictory Messages
Credibility Gap
Degrees of Concern
93/7
Most Important Message
Effective Communication

Discussion of Meanings

1. What is the definition of communications?
2. Explain the A.I.M.E. model. Please define each of the variables in the model?
3. Why is our behavior more credible than our words?
4. Why is appropriateness important when you communicate? What are some ways that students communicate inappropriately to professors? What are some ways that professors communicate inappropriately to students?
5. List as many things as you can think of that you communicate non-verbally.
6. In the author's view, what is the single most important message that people should communicate? Why?
7. What are the different audiences that you communicate with?
8. What is the distinction between audiences that have a high level of involvement with you and a low level of involvement with you?
9. What are some examples of contradictory behavior? Why is contradictory behavior so problematic for you?
10. Explain the 93/7 Rule that Merhabian and Weiner discovered in their research.
11. Explain what Watzlawick, Beavin, and Jackson meant with the communication axiom, "One cannot not communicate."
12. What were the students trying to communicate in their e-mails? What did they actually communicate?
13. What evidence do students leave behind about their true nature when they communicate?
14. Why is sending contradictory or conflicting messages so problematic?
15. Do you communicate appropriately to the different audiences that experience you? Explain your answer.

Communications Personal Policy Contract

To help you achieve your behavioral goals, you will be writing them down to create Personal Policy Contracts like the one below. By signing and dating the Personal Policy Contract, it becomes an obligation to yourself that cannot be broken.

Communication Goals

Goals

Communication goal(s) that will guide how I communicate in college:

_____

_____

_____

_____

Personal Policies

Personal policies I will follow when I communicate with others:

_____

_____

_____

_____

Public Commitments

Public commitments that I will make to regularly measure how I am doing regarding my communication goals and personal policies. I will send my goals, personal policies, and quick weekly progress reports to a supportive friend and the professor.

_____

_____

_____

_____

Signature: _____ **Date:** _____

Practice True/False Self-Test
(Explain if false)

Is each of the following statements *True* or *False*? Circle the best answer. If your answer is false, briefly describe why. (Hint: All of the answers are false)

For example:

1. The trust definition for Consideration is "Trust a person to show a thoughtful concern for others."

    True or *False*

    The answer is false because "Trust a person to show thoughtful concern for others" is the trust definition for Caring not Consideration.

---

1. A behavioral occurrence of absenteeism is evidence of a behavior-related issue.

    True or False

2. The 4 variables in the A.I.M.E. model are Audience, Interest, Messages, and Evidence.

    True or False

3. In the author's view, the single most important message that you can communicate to others is "loyalty."

    True or False

4. Communication theorists Sacco and Vanzetti coined the communication axiom, "One cannot not communicate."

    True or False

5. The opposite of audience involvement is audience concern.   True or False

6. Interest looks at whether or not an audience type cares much about the outcomes of your behavioral choices.   True or False

7. Honesty is revealed when our words and behaviors are in alignment.   True or False

8. Gathering detailed information on the characteristics of audience types will put you in a better position to gauge the sincerity of your communication messages when you interact with others.   True or False

9. Communications is defined as *"the process that creates agreement between people."*   True or False

10. In their research entitled Decoding of Inconsistent Messages, Mehrabian and Wiener found that people communicate only 38% *without* words?   True or False

To Sum Up

Unit 2 focused on communication.

First, and most importantly, you learned that 93% of what we communicate has nothing to do with words. Our actions speak much louder than our words. You learned that good communication creates understanding between people and that communicating well involves conveying messages appropriately to others.

Second, you were introduced to the A.I.M.E. model. The A.I.M.E. model is the framework within which you can identify the different audiences that you interact with, define the characteristics unique to each audience type, outline your level of involvement with each audience type, identify the messages that each audience type will be looking for from you, and analyze how your actions are evidence that substantiate claims that you make about yourself. You also learned about the importance of communicating trust with all of your actions and words.

Third, you were asked to take a communication effectiveness self-assessment and then to transfer the results to the behavior-mapping table, and then to write down some tiny habits that you can use to help you change the way you communicate.

Lastly, to help you achieve your behavioral goals, you were asked to create a Communication Personal Policy Contract for yourself. By signing and dating the Personal Policy Contract, it became an obligation to yourself that cannot be broken.

Unit 3

Choice

Understanding Choice

"We are our choices."

~ Jean-Paul Sartre

Communication is a choice. Commitment is a choice. Caring is a choice. Coping is a choice. Choosing is a choice. At what point do people become responsible for their choices? At what age should conscious decision-making start and acting on impulse stop? As stated in the introduction, infants are all impulse. They act and react based on the sensations in their bodies without considering consequences. They coo when they are happy and content; they cry when they are uncomfortable.

As people mature, we become aware of how our bodily sensations affect our behavior. We begin to understand cause and effect. We learn that impulsive behavior has consequences. Over time, we learn to moderate impulses based on the effect that they have on others and ourselves. When children consider situations and bodily sensations and comprehend the meaning of the circumstances in which they find themselves, they become aware of themselves within the situations that they find themselves.

Continuing with this logic, when children consciously consider situational factors and then make thoughtful choices from different alternatives, they affect the direction of their lives. The same is true for adults.

Choices are the forces that move people in one direction or another.

Life happens in real-time, and every moment is different. The ability to accurately comprehend what is happening in real-time is critically important for successful decision-making. In fact, accurately comprehending the meaning of the present is arguably the most important skillset that one can develop. How can one begin to understand future consequences if one does not correctly comprehend his or her present situation? The late American author David Foster Wallace powerfully pointed out in his 2005 Commencement Speech to Kenyon College graduates: The ability to clearly see that which is in plain view in front of each of us is sometimes the hardest thing to do.

"There are these two young fish swimming along and they happen to meet an older fish swimming the other way, who nods at them and says 'Morning, boys. How's the water?' And the two young fish swim on for a bit, and then eventually one of them looks over at the other and said, 'What the hell is water?'" [26]

---

[26] "This is Water" by David Foster Wallace delivered 2005 commencement speech to the graduating students of Kenyon College: listen to attribution starting 0:17 at (https://www.youtube.com/watch?v=8CrOL-ydFMI)

If one cannot clearly comprehend the world in which he or she lives (or swims), one may have difficulty comprehending the future consequences of his or her choices. Because the trajectory and outcome of everyone's life is largely the result of one's choices, everyone should be able to clearly see the *water* in which he or she swims.

To help ensure that choices are informed and sound, it is important to consciously analyze circumstances prior to making decisions. If conscious analysis is not done in real-time, prior to making a decision, a person is not operating in real-time. Rather, he or she is on autopilot … giving up control of that which flies the plane. Situations that require real-time cognition, analysis, and problem solving must be informed by real-time information because the information is what differentiates decision-making from guesswork.

So, how do you make good choices? The ability to make good decisions is a result of proactive, careful analysis of all available information relating to the matter requiring a decision. Relevant factors that are fundamental to good decision-making are:

1. Accurately assessing potential future consequences of decisions on one's life.
2. Consistently prioritizing more consequential matters ahead of less consequential matters.
3. Understanding what values are important to you and the role values and ethics play in decision-making.
4. Defining the type of person you want to be.
5. Accurately assessing or understanding your current reality.

These factors become the framework within which information can be gathered, organized, and analyzed when making a decision. They play an essential part in determining risk and the best course of action. Decisions made without clearly understanding these variables are more likely to produce bad results. Again, the data is what separates sound decision-making from guesswork.

Of course, we can ignore the data and make decisions based solely on impulse. But, we should not be surprised, then, when our lives deteriorate into a uniquely worsened states that are our own doing. Although hindsight is twenty-twenty, the formation of judgments and decisions based on inaccurate or inconclusive information and/or impulsiveness are often at the heart of most poor decision-making and regret.

Understanding Consequences

We make choices every minute of every day. We choose when we get up, when we go to bed, what we eat, how much we eat, whom to associate with, when to exercise. Our decisions have consequences. We can think conceptually of decision-making as an …

organized and intentional approach to assessing the consequential effects of choices on one's life.

The main goal of decision-making is to increase the probability that the beneficial consequences chosen will be greater than the costly consequences not chosen. So decision-making is fundamentally a cost benefit analysis. The benefits associated with decision-making can be called *beneficial consequences*. Beneficial consequences can be defined as the potential impact (good or bad) that is received when an opportunity is chosen. Whereas the costs associated with a particular choice are called *costly consequences*. Costly consequences can be defined as the potential impact that is lost when an opportunity is not chosen.

The main goal of this consequential *cost benefit analysis* is to increase the probability that the positive impact of decisions made (beneficial consequences) is greater than the future consequences of decisions not made (costly consequences). The ability to correctly judge the potential future consequences on one's life is fundamental to good decision-making.

Some decision-making opportunities will be more consequential than others because they have the power to produce life-changing effects (good and bad) on our lives. In general, decision-making opportunities that have more significant consequences (i.e. the power to affect the outcome of our lives) should be prioritized ahead of opportunities that are less consequential. Good decision-making, then, can be thought of as an intentional prioritization and selection of more consequential matters ahead of less consequential matters. To do otherwise, to prioritize less consequential matters ahead of more consequential matters, is bad judgment and, by logical extension, poor decision-making. So good judgment can be defined as …

the ability to consistently prioritize more consequential matters ahead of less consequential matters in decision-making.

What are the distinctions between consequential and inconsequential matters? Decisions-making can be grouped into four distinct levels of priority: Severely Consequential, Consequential, Mildly Consequential, and Inconsequential. The priority levels and definitions of each decision-making matter are defined in (Table 2.1) on the following page.

Self-Management:
Understanding, Communicating and Assessing
Behavioral Competency, 3rd Edition
Gian Paolo Roma - © 2019 - All Rights Reserved

Decision-Making Prioritization Framework

Priority	Definitions	Matter (s)
Severely Consequential	Failure to prioritize these matters ahead of all other matters can take away your ability to make choices.	• Health • Safety and Security • Freedom
Consequential	Failure to prioritize these matters ahead of less consequential matters can *hurt* your ability to live the life that you want to live.	• Character • Relationships
Mildly Consequential	These matters can *improve* your ability to live the life that you want to live.	• Free time • Material possessions • Prosperity
Inconsequential	Everything else.	

Table 2.1

Because we have unrestrained freedom of choice, we have the *power and right* to do what we please. We have the power and right to make good choices, and we have the power and right to make bad choices. Viewed through the lens of this framework, the quality of an individual's decision-making and judgment becomes clear. Although decision-making usually involves some kind of ambiguity, it's safe to say those individuals that demonstrate patterns of *independently, willingly, and consistently* prioritizing more consequential matters *ahead* of less consequential matters communicate common-sense and good judgment. While this logic may not be true in every circumstance, such as heroism, the logic does hold up in most situations.

The opposite is also true. Individuals that seem to chronically prioritize less consequential matters ahead of more consequential matters communicate a lack of judgment that may expose themselves and others to unnecessary risks and problems. For example, if an individual prioritizes texting a friend while driving ahead of safety, he or she prioritizes social matters ahead of safety matters. While the most important matter in driving is safety, today, the number one reason for driving fatalities is distracted driving.

Self-Management:
Understanding, Communicating and Assessing
Behavioral Competency, 3rd Edition
Gian Paolo Roma - © 2019 - All Rights Reserved

Think About It

Why do people prioritize less consequential matters ahead of more consequential matters? Explain your answer.

_____

_____

_____

Severely Consequential Matters: Health, Safety, Security, and Freedom

We see, touch, taste, hear, and smell our world, experience life, and exist within our bodies and minds. The quality of our existence depends on our physical person being free and in good working order. Because we seem to exist within our physical being, matters involving our health, safety, security, and freedom must be prioritized above all other matters. When we are healthy, safe, secure, and free we have the opportunity to make choices without hindrance. If our personal choices compromise our health, safety, security, or freedom, we render all others matters in our lives irrelevant. (i.e. if we are ill, dead, or in jail, we cannot make choices for ourselves any more).

Think About It

Why do people smoke, text while driving, and commit crimes if they can destroy their own ability to make all others choices? Explain your answer.

_____

_____

_____

Consequential Matters: Character and Relationships

When severely consequential matters are not in play, choices affecting our character and relationships become the priority. Because we have the freedom and power to do as we please, we have the ability to influence our future. Not only can our choices impact our very existence; they can also shape our character and relationships. If in our pursuit of life, liberty, and happiness we damage our own character and relationships, we may hurt our ability to live the life that we want to live. That's because we define ourselves by the decisions that we make. And those very same decisions define us to others.

Think About It

Can freedom from external restraint (being told what to do by others) hurt our ability to live the life that we want to live? If so, how? Explain your answer.

_____

_____

_____

Mildly Consequential: Material Possessions, Free Time, and Prosperity

When we are free, safe, healthy, and secure and our character and relationships are harmonious, matters that can enhance our well-being may become a priority. Matters involving the quantity and quality of our material possessions, free time, and prosperity, can improve our ability to live the life we want to live. Although material possessions, free time, and prosperity are important, it would be unwise to prioritize them ahead of more consequential matters because without our health, safety, security, character, and relationships we cannot fully enjoy them anyway.

Think About It

What's more important freedom or happiness? Explain your answer.

_____

_____

_____

Mistake or Bad Decision?

"Learn from the mistakes of others. You can't live long enough to make them all yourself."

~ Eleanor Roosevelt

"Bad decisions are not mistakes. Bad decisions are choices. People don't choose to make mistakes."[27] Selecting the wrong answer on a test is a mistake; not studying for that test is a bad decision. The mistake was something you did without intention; the bad decision was made intentionally.[28]

Your intentions are ambitions that guide your decision-making in the present.

Intentions are different than goals. Goals are future-oriented ambitions and concerned with future states of being. Intentions, on the other hand, are now-oriented ambitions or desires and concerned with current states-of-being. Although spontaneity is sometimes fun, most bad judgment occurs when current intentions (and decision-making) are not in alignment with future goals. When people knowingly make decisions in the present that are not aligned with their desired future goals, poor judgment is revealed.

People often use the word mistake to avoid taking responsibility for their own bad decision-making. For example:

- Two students missed an exam because they said that they got a flat tire. Their professor called them individually into his office and asked them one simple question: "Which tire was it?" The students both gave different answers. When they got caught lying, they said that they "made a mistake."

- Two students had the exact same *wrong* mathematical answers on every question of an exam. When they were caught cheating, they said that they "made a mistake."

- A student was chronically absent or late to her class. When she was dropped from the class for poor attendance, she said that she "made a mistake."

- A student never did his homework. When he got academically dismissed from college for poor grades, he said that he "made a mistake."

---

[27] As stated in a conversation with Corinne Elisa Roma, August 2016.

[28] Milburn, Joshua Fields and Nicodemus, Ryan, http://www.theminimalists.com/mistakes/.

Mistakes and bad decisions are both painful because they involve learning. Mistakes and bad decisions are …

the doors through which ignorance enters and exits our bodies.

We learn what to do and what not to do by making mistakes and bad decisions. We learn to walk by falling down. Kids want to stay standing because falling hurts. The pain *is* the lesson. People that try to reduce or eliminate the pain of bad decision-making by reclassifying bad judgment as a mistake may not remember the lesson, which brings to mind the following quote, "Those who cannot remember the past are condemned to repeat it."[29]

Think About It

In your opinion, what's more important for success in college: good behavioral decision-making or being highly intelligent? Please explain your answer.

_____

_____

_____

_____

---

[29] Santayana, George, *The Life of Reason*, 1905.

Anatomy of a Bad Decision

If one was to study the root causes of most bad decisions, one would discover that there are three main factors that contribute to poor judgment. These factors are depicted by the bad judgment model (*Figure 2.1*).[30]

Bad Judgment Model

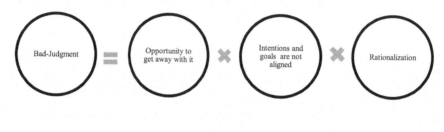

Figure 2.1

The first factor in the bad-judgment model is *opportunity*. For one to consciously make a bad decision, one must first believe that he or she has the opportunity to get away with it. College is the first time that many students experience freedom and independence from parental supervision, and function as autonomous self-managing adults. With adult freedom comes adult responsibility. Some students may believe that they will not get caught or suffer any consequences when they don't study or take notes or attend class.

Think About It

Can students that self-manage ever have the opportunity to get away with not going to class or doing their homework or cheating? Please explain your answer.

_____

_____

_____

_____

---

[30] Adapted from Donald Cressey and Edwin Sutherland article in the *Journal of Accountancy* entitled "Why Do Trusted Persons Commit Fraud? A Social-Psychological Study of Defalcators". November 1951

The second factor that contributes to bad judgment is a failure to align behavioral intentions with behavioral goals. As discussed previously, behavioral goals are long-term ambitions or desires that are concerned with future states of being. Whereas, behavioral intentions are short-term ambitions that guide our choices in the present. Sometimes the root cause of bad decision-making is that people fail to align short-term ambitions with long-term goals.

For instance, a college student might have a long-term goal of graduating from college, and at the very same time intentionally do not take notes or attend class or read assignments or do homework.

Think About It

Why do some students fail to align their behavioral intentions with their behavioral goals? How can you reduce the likelihood that this will happen to you? Please explain your answer.

_____

_____

_____

_____

The third variable that contributes to bad judgment is *rationalization*. In order to justify bad judgment, people often rationalize their behavior to sooth their consciences. For example, some students feel justified in cheating because they argue that everybody else is doing it.

Think About It

Rationalization is the use of weak and superficially believable arguments to justify choices that are difficult to accept or to make them seem *okay*. In what ways do students justify not attending class or walking in late or not doing their homework or cheating?

_____

_____

_____

_____

Understanding Your Values and Ethics

*"He who lets the world, or his own portion of it, choose his plan of life for him,
has no need of any other faculty than the ape-like one of imitation.
He who chooses his plan for himself employs all his faculties."[31]*

~ John Stuart Mill

The choices that you make reveal your values. They reveal what is important to you. Values are the underlying set of principles (or rules) that govern your thinking, judgment, behavior, and ultimately, every choice that you make.

Values inform your opinions about what is right, wrong, and just in the world.

In general, decision-making that encourages respect and dignity in yourself and others is universally regarded as honorable, virtuous, and morally good. The byproduct of morally sound decision-making is trust.

In contrast, decisions that undermine individual dignity and respect result in mistrust of some kind. Keep in mind that a person can communicate trust to one audience type, but not to others. Behaviorally competent people try to behave in a trustworthy manner to everyone that they encounter, not just to a select few.

Choices involve values. Many situations are complex and involve more than one value. Ethics relates to your choice of values when you make a decision. In ethics …

you must choose between competing values by ranking one value over other values.

Some choices are easy and some are not. Ethical decision-making forces you to select one value over all other values and possibly compromise beliefs that are important to you. These choices can affect how you see yourself and influence the way others see you too. When the choice is difficult, you may feel caught between a rock and a hard place. This is called an ethical dilemma.

---

[31] Mill, J. S., & In Rapaport, E. (1859). *On liberty.*

Think about it

Questions 1: Would you lie under oath in a court of law to protect a friend after you saw him do something illegal if you knew that you would be fined or go to jail? If you knew that you wouldn't get caught, would your answer change? Please explain your answer.

_____

_____

_____

_____

_____

_____

Question 2: What would you do if a cashier accidentally gave you an extra $1.00 in change? Would you give it back, or would you keep the extra buck? Explain your answer.

_____

_____

_____

_____

_____

_____

What values are important to you?

Take a few minutes and think about the people in your life. In the spaces provided below, identify the person you most admire. Why do you admire that person? After you have figured out whom you admire and why, try to identify a person that you don't admire. Why don't you admire him or her? Is your opinion of that person the result of his or her actions or words?

Who is a person you admire *most*? _____

What are the personal qualities that you admire most about that person?

_____

_____

_____

Who is a person you admire *least*? _____

What are the personal qualities that you dislike about that person?

_____

_____

_____

In this exercise, we have identified many different behavioral traits, some admirable and some not so admirable. If a person communicates that he or she is a liar, bigot, disloyal, lazy, unreliable, mean, or abusive, he or she will become defined by those behavioral qualities. By contrast, those who are consistently honest, loyal, fair-minded, hard-working, reliable, and respectful of others, tend to be trusted and respected by others. You expect people to behave in certain ways. One person lives up to your expectations and the other does not.

Just as you expect others to behave in certain ways, others will have expectations of you. They will be looking for behavioral evidence that they can confidently rely on you. People will be more apt to help and support you if they admire and trust you. Years from now, if your family, friends, and associates are asked who they most admire and least admire, which list will you be on? If you believe that you will be on the admired list, what behavioral evidence can you provide to substantiate your belief?

What type of person do you want to be?

As discussed earlier, your words and actions communicate facts and information about yourself that influence how others see you. Your choices communicate what is distinctive about you. Your choices continually transmit information about your values, ethics, judgment, manner, emotions, friendliness, interest, desire, motivation, attitude, aptitude, dependability, and work ethic. In short, your choices reveal your character and true nature. As the philosopher Jean-Paul Sartre wrote …

"We are our choices."

How you are perceived is largely a consequence of your behavioral choices. In life, the choices you make about how you say and do things, how hard you work, how nice you are to others, how dependable you are, how you deal with your problems are all plain and clear for others to see, understand, and interpret. As such, your choices define you to others. Not only that, your own self-image will be shaped in part by those very same choices.

Making decisions that are good for you begins with an understanding of the type of person you want to be. If you want to be a trustworthy person, then your choices should be worthy of trust. For example, if you don't show up to your classes, your poor attendance will characterize you to your professors as being less committed than those that show up. Showing up to class is a *choice of action* that others will use to describe the type of person that they see and/or experience. The type of person you want to be is a destination or endpoint toward which your judgment and choices should take you. In the same way that you cannot chart a course to an unknown destination, you cannot make the best choices for yourself if you do not know the type of person that you want to be. Do you understand the behavioral traits that define your character?

Think about it

Try to imagine that all of your college professors had a meeting about you and that you could eavesdrop on that meeting. What would you *hope* they would say about you? Using the list of positive qualities listed in the most admired and least admired exercise, please list (in order of importance) the top three personal qualities (using only one word) that you would *hope* your professors would say about you. What you *hope* they would say might not be the same as what they would actually say. Only list the personal qualities that you hope that they would say about you that would bring you the most joy. If the words below are not descriptive enough for you, please list other words that you would hope others would use to describe you.

1. Considerate	13. Accountable	25. Strong	37. Cooperative
2. Interested	14. Forgiving	26. Stable	38. Stamina
3. Hard working	15. Honorable	27. Survivor	39. Ambitious
4. Contentious	16. Kind	28. Energetic	40. Determined
5. Open minded	17. Committed	29. Charismatic	41. Trustworthy
6. Honest	18. Competent	30. Responsible	42. Punctual
7. Courageous	19. Happy	31. Motivated	43. Competitive
8. Modest	20. Graceful	32. Dignified	44. Humble
9. Safety conscious	21. Adaptable	33. Prepared	45. Helpful
10. Objective	22. Status conscious	34. Empathic	46. Loyal
11. Reliable	23. Fair minded	35. Excitable	47. Sincere
12. Secure	24. Friendly	36. Passionate	48. Cool

1. _____

2. _____

3. _____

Character Statement

Next, using just one sentence, starting with "I would hope they would say that I was …", please write down your character statement or personal policy that you would like to guide your behavioral conduct and decision-making going forward. QUICK TIP: What would you like your friends, family and colleagues to say about you at your funeral? What would make you feel content?

I would hope they would say that I was …

_____

It is never too late to become the person that you want to become. How you choose to interact with the rest of the world is up to you. Your own daily choices will determine your character and the type of person you become. Choose wisely because choices communicate your character to others.

Understanding Your Reality

"We cannot change the cards we are dealt, just how we play the hand."

~ Randy Pausch

As discussed at the beginning of this unit, the outcome of each person's life will be largely the result of the choices he or she has made. If one considers the type of person he or she wants to be as the *end-point* of our decision-making, one must next accurately define his or her *start-point,* to figure out how he or she is going to become that person. For example, if a pilot wants to fly to Los Angeles, the best route to get there depends on where the pilot starts. In order for you to reach your desired *end-point*, you must know your *start-point*, where your decision-making must always begin.

Other factors such as safety, weather, engine, and air traffic problems may also influence pilot decision-making along the way to the end-point or destination. For example, pilots can change course or altitude to avoid severe turbulence if they know beforehand about severe weather conditions. The line between the two points may be straight or meandering depending on what is encountered along the way. Similarly, by understanding as much as possible our start-point or current reality *before* we make decisions, we can anticipate things before they happen and make adjustments along the way to our end-point. How you get to your end-point is your choice. Try to remember that decision-making without accurate information about your current situation is nothing more than guesswork. It is like flying a plane on a foggy night without instrument gauges, or *flying blind.*

Seeing your current reality clearly is much like seeing the picture on the box of a jigsaw puzzle emerge with the assembly of each puzzle piece. You try to put together as many small, interlocking pieces of information as you can. Each piece of information has on it a small part of the picture about your current reality. The more pieces of reality that you put together, the clearer the picture of your current reality will become.

Unlike jigsaw puzzles, however, decisions are usually made without having a complete picture of your reality of a situation. The goal is to assemble enough information so that the picture of your current reality begins to emerge. This need to be done *before* the actual decision is made.

If information arrives after a decision has been made, it cannot inform the decision. Therefore, good decision-making requires information be timely. If the information is timely, then the next requirement for good decision-making is correct information. Good choices depend on correct information. Choices are only as good as the information that informs them. If information is incorrect, the resulting decision will probably be bad, unless luck intervenes. It is a good idea to verify the correctness of the information supplied whenever you are making a decision. This is true especially when decisions are critical or when the information source is unreliable.

Bad information begets bad choices.

Or as Sophocles stated, "No enemy is worse than bad advice."[32]

If the information is both timely and correct, then the last requirement for making good decisions is to make sure that you have as much information as needed to make the decision. Making decisions without having enough information is called conclusion jumping, and can be just as error-prone as decisions made with bad information. The saying is "on your mark, get set, go," not "on your mark, go, get set."

At what point can you feel comfortable making decisions? If you can begin to see how the decision will affect your reality one day, one week, one month, one year, or five years out, then you increase the probability that the outcome of your decision-making will be as you predicted. If you cannot begin to see how the decision will affect your future reality, then you are probably *conclusion-jumping* and need to gather more information.

To see if your judgment and decision-making are consistently in your best interest, please take a few minutes to complete the self-assessment, *Choice/Judgment Effectiveness: A Self-Assessment,* on the next page.

---

[32] 496--406 bc, Greek dramatist; author of seven extant tragedies: Ajax, Antigone, Oedipus Rex, Trachiniae, Electra, Philoctetes, and Oedipus at Colonus

Choice/Judgment Effectiveness: A Self-Assessment

Below Expectations	Meets Expectations	Role Model
Even with guidance, fails to provide evidence *(verbal, written, and behavioral)* that their actions and words demonstrate good judgment and/or aligned with audience expectations. Even with guidance, fails to provide evidence of these behaviors and is unwilling to prioritize important matters ahead of unimportant matters.	With guidance, provides evidence *(verbal, written, and behavioral)* that their actions and words demonstrate good judgment and aligned with audience expectations. With guidance, provides evidence of these behaviors and is willing to prioritize important matters ahead of unimportant matters.	Independently provides evidence *(verbal, written, and behavioral)* that their actions and words demonstrate good judgment and/or aligned with audience expectations. Willingly provides evidence of these behaviors and can be trusted to prioritize important matters ahead of unimportant matters.

Using the Behavioral Observation Scale below as a guide, for each statement on the following page write in the rating column the number corresponding to the degree to which you consistently exhibit the behavior described in the statement. Note, there are no right or wrong answers. All that is important is that you indicate how consistently you exhibit the behavior described in the action statement.

Use the following Behavioral Observation Scale:

5 = Almost always performs as described by the Role Model standard.

4 = Sometimes performs as described by the Role Model standard and sometimes perform as described by the Meets Expectations standards.

3 = Almost always performs as described by the Meets Expectations standard.

2 = Sometimes performs as described by the Meets Expectations standard and sometimes perform as described by the Below Expectations standards.

1 = Almost always performs as described by the Below Expectations standard.

	Action Statement	Rating
1	I spend between 10 and 20 hours, outside of class, on my schoolwork (e.g. doing homework, studying, or preparing for tests).	
2	I challenge myself to practice and understand subjects that I find difficult or I do not understand well.	
3	I get all of my work done, no matter how long it takes.	
4	I go out only after my academic work is completed.	
5	I don't miss class, am always on time, and remain in class.	
6	I am ready to work and prepared for every class.	
7	I earn high grades (A's or B's) or marks in my classes.	
8	I am comfortable and like communicating with and meeting new people.	
9	When I do poorly or when I don't understand something, I try harder by spending more time on that subject.	
10	I can juggle large amounts of responsibility at school, work, and home and still produce high quality work.	
11	I can figure out how to do almost any subject, if I put my mind and effort into it.	
12	I try to be polite, even when I don't need to be.	
13	I consider the other person and can find common ground when I am in a dispute.	
14	I am careful not to harm people with my words, even when I get frustrated.	
15	I challenge myself to help bring order to different situations, even when things do not go my way.	
16	I am interested in what others have to say, even when I disagree with them.	
17	I accurately assess potential future consequences of decisions on my life.	
18	I prioritize consequential matters before less consequential matters when I make decisions.	
19	I align my decision-making with the type of person I want to be.	
20	I accurately assess and understand my current reality before I make decisions.	

Now transfer your answers for each statement into the corresponding space in the table below.

Self-Management:
Understanding, Communicating and Assessing
Behavioral Competency, 3rd Edition
Gian Paolo Roma - © 2019 - All Rights Reserved

Choice/Judgment: Behavior-Mapping Table

Item	Variable	Behavior	Behavior Average	Behavior Rating
1	Commitment	Time		
2	Commitment	Deliberate Practice		
3	Commitment	Effort		
4	Commitment	Delayed Gratification		
5	Commitment	Reliability		
6	Commitment	Preparedness		
7	Commitment	Quality		
8	Coping	Change		
9	Coping	Adversity		
10	Coping	Capacity		
11	Coping	Capability		
12	Caring	Courteousness		
13	Caring	Negotiating		
14	Caring	Patience		
15	Caring	Helpfulness		
16	Caring	Listening		
17	Choice	Ethical		
18	Choice	Judgment		
19	Choice	Character		
20	Choice	Data/Information		
Average				

Average = ∑ of Behavior Rating/20: [ ]

Greater than 4: If your average is between 4 and 5, you are a good decision-maker, prioritize important matters ahead of unimportant matters, and require little guidance to use good judgment and make good decisions.

Between 3 and 4: If your average is greater than 3 but less than 4, with guidance, you are a good decision-maker.

Less than 3: If your average is less than 3, with guidance you might use good judgment. But occasionally, even with guidance, you fail to do the right thing.

Take your behavior averages for this section, calculate the new average of averages, and input that information into the Employability Profile on the following page.

Employability Profile   Student Name _____   Home School _____

Recommended for Employment [Select]	Total Work-Based Learning Hours [Select]	Portfolio Completed [Select]	Passed State/National Assessment [Select]
1	2	3	4	5

Below Expectations

Even with guidance, fails to provide evidence *(verbal, written, and behavioral)* that they communicate appropriately, prioritize important matters ahead of unimportant matters, show thoughtful concern for others, follow through and meet obligations, and adapt effectively to difficult, changing, and complex circumstances.

Even with guidance, fails to provide evidence of these behaviors and is unwilling to work on trust and responsibility.

Meets Expectations

With guidance, provides evidence *(verbal, written, and behavioral)* that they communicate appropriately, prioritize important matters ahead of unimportant matters, show thoughtful concern for others, follow through and meet obligations, and adapt effectively to difficult, changing, and complex circumstances.

With guidance, provides evidence of these behaviors and is willing to work on trust responsibility.

Role Model

Independently provides evidence *(verbal, written, and behavioral)* that they communicate appropriately, prioritize important matters ahead of unimportant matters, show thoughtful concern for others, follow through and meet obligations, and adapt effectively to difficult, changing, and complex circumstances.

Willingly provides evidence of these behaviors and can be trusted with responsibility.

Where:

5 = Almost always performs as described by the "Role Model" standard.
4 = Sometimes performs as described by the "Role Model" standard and sometimes performs as described by the "Meets Expectations" standard.
3 = Almost always performs as described by the "Meets Expectations" standard.
2 = Sometimes performs as described by the "Meets Expectations" standard and sometimes performs as described by the "Below Expectations" standard.
1 = Almost always performs as described by the "Below Expectations" standard.

Communication
Trust a person to convey messages appropriately to others.

- Audience
- Involvement
- Message
- Evidence
- COMMUNICATION MEAN

Choices
Trust a person to prioritize important matters ahead of unimportant matters.

- Communication
- Commitment
- Coping
- Caring
- CHOICE MEAN

Commitment
Trust a person to follow through and meet obligations.

- Dependability — Attendance
- Dependability — Accountability
- Dependability — Contribution
- Hard Work — Time — Deliberate Practice
- Hard Work — Delayed Gratification
- Hard Work — Energy
- Hard Work — Effort — Determination
- Hard Work — Effort — Stamina
- Quality — Measure of Excellence
- Quality — Continuous Improvement
- COMMITMENT MEAN

Coping
Trust a person to handle and adapt effectively to difficult, changing, and complex circumstances

- Coping — Change — Demonstration
- Coping — Adversity — Self-Awareness
- Coping — Adversity — Self-Restraint
- Coping — Adversity — Self-Improvement
- Coping — Complexity — Capability
- Coping — Complexity — Capacity
- COPING MEAN

Caring
Trust a person to show thoughtful concern for others.

- Caring — Consideration — Listening
- Caring — Consideration — Courtesy
- Caring — Consideration — Respectful
- Caring — Concern — Cooperation
- Caring — Concern — Helpful
- Caring — Concern — Compromise
- Caring — Conscientious — Thoughtful
- Caring — Conscientious — Careful
- Caring — Conscientious — Fair
- CARING MEAN

BEHAVIORAL COMPETENCY RATING (BCR) (MEAN OF MEANS)

Think about It

You will define yourself by the decisions that you make, and those very same decisions will define you to others. The Choice/Judgment Mapping Table tells if you prioritize important matters ahead of less important matters, or not. What is your average?

_____

_____

_____

_____

Changing Habits

How can you employ Fogg's Behavior Model tiny habits described earlier to improve the quality of your decision-making?

Please take a few moments and try to come up with one tiny decision-making habit that you can use to help you make better decisions. As you think about changing your habits, think about framing the tiny habit in the following format suggested by Dr. Fogg: "After I (insert existing behavior), I will (insert new tiny behavior)."

After I _____,

I will _____.

Appendices

Located at the back of the book are two appendices that have been designed to help you gather information about college and about yourself. Specifically, in Appendix I, you will find the current U.S. Department of Labor data about the effect that a college education has on career earnings and employment. By gathering this real-world data, you will be better able to see for yourself the value of graduating from college.

In Appendix II you will gather information about the external realities (opportunities and threats) influencing your world today. In addition, you will define your own unique internal realities (strengths and weaknesses) that exist within you. By understanding your internal and external realities, you will be in a better position to judge the appropriateness of your decision-making.

Important Terms

If you learn to understand these words and phrases thoroughly – if you can explain each one and use them correctly – your ability to make sound choices will become much easier for you.

Choices
Decision-Making
Good Judgment
Consequences
Cost Benefit Analysis
Beneficial Consequences
Costly Consequences
Intentions vs. Goals

Decision-Making Prioritization Framework
Mistakes vs. Bad Decisions
Anatomy of a Bad Decision
Values
Ethics
Admirable
Reality

Discussion of Meanings

1. If you could see the impact of your choices on your future, would that knowledge affect your choices today?
2. Why do people make bad decisions? Discuss the differences between good judgment and bad judgment.
3. Can adults behave like children? What are the main behavioral differences between children and adults?
4. What two kinds of consequences have you learned about in this unit?
5. Perform a cost benefit analysis of going to college.
6. Name, define, and provide examples of the four levels of the decision-making prioritization framework.
7. What are some practical uses of the decision-making prioritization framework for college students?
8. What is the main point of thinking about behavioral decision-making as a cost benefit analysis?
9. Why do people make mistakes? Discuss the differences between mistakes and bad decisions.
10. How do people communicate their values? What is the difference between values and ethics?
11. What is an ethical dilemma?
12. Is it in your interest to demonstrate values that are generally accepted to be admirable? Why?
13. Do you interact with people that you do not trust? If so, why?
14. What was the main point of the "most admired/least-admired" exercise?
15. What are some of the challenges that you face today that your parents did not face?

Choices Personal Policy Contract

To help you achieve your behavioral goals, you will be writing them down to create Personal Policy Contracts like the one below. By signing and dating the Personal Policy Contract, it becomes an obligation to yourself that cannot be broken.

Choice Goals

Goals　　　　　Choice goal(s) that will guide my decision-making in college:

_____

_____

_____

_____

Personal Policies　　Personal policies I will follow when I make choices:

_____

_____

_____

_____

Public Commitments　　Public commitments that I will make to regularly measure how I am doing regarding my choice goals and personal policies. I will send my goals, personal policies, and quick weekly progress reports to a supportive friend and the professor.

_____

_____

_____

_____

Signature: _____　**Date:** _____

Practice True/False Self-Test
(Explain if false)

Is each of the following statements *True* or *False*? Circle the best answer. If your answer is false, briefly describe why. (Hint: All of the answers are false)

For example:

1. The trust definition for Consideration is "Trust a person to show a thoughtful concern for others."   True or *False*

   The answer is false because "Trust a person to show thoughtful concern for others" is the trust definition for Caring not Consideration.

---

1. Mistakes and bad decisions are essentially the same.   True or False

2. Examples of severely consequential matters defined in the decision-making prioritization framework are your character and relationships.   True or False

3. The difference between good decision-making from guesswork is intuition.   True or False

4. Intentions and goals are the same thing.   True or False

5. Morality is a prioritization of a person's values in decision-making. In morality, one value is chosen ahead of all other important values when a decision is made.

True or False

6. Values are the forces that move people in one direction or another.

True or False

7. Logic is ability to consistently prioritize more consequential matters ahead of less consequential matters in decision-making.

True or False

8. Morality relate to the prioritization of your values when you make a decision.

True or False

9. Not studying for a test is a mistake.

True or False

10. In the Decision-Making Prioritization Framework, character and relationships are defined as severely consequential matters.

True or False

To Sum Up

Unit 3 focused on choices.

First, the most significant concept you learned in Unit 2 is that your choices define your character. You learned that decision-making is an organized and intentional approach to assessing the consequential effects of choices on one's life, and just as you *expect* others to behave in certain ways towards you, others will have expectations of you. They will be looking for behavioral evidence that they can trust you.

Second, you learned that making good choices involves: accurately assessing potential future consequences of decisions on one's life, consistently prioritizing more consequential matters ahead of less consequential matters, understanding what values are important to you and the role values and ethics play in decision-making, defining the type of person you want to be, and, accurately assessing or understanding your current reality. These five functions provide the framework within which good decision-making occurs. The overall goal is to gather enough information to feel comfortable estimating the consequential effects of decisions on your life.

Third, you were introduced to a new Decision-Making Prioritization Framework that can help you judge the quality of your decision-making and judgment. Ultimately, if you *independently, willingly, and consistently* demonstrate behavioral patterns of prioritizing more consequential matters *ahead* of less consequential matters, you will communicate common sense and good judgment.

Fourth, you learned about the distinction between mistakes and bad decision-making and the role that values and ethics play in the decision-making process.

Fifth, you were asked to take a choice/judgment effectiveness self-assessment and then transfer the results to the behavior-mapping table, and then write down some tiny habits that you can use to help insure that you make sound decisions.

Lastly, to help you achieve your behavioral goals, you were asked to create a Personal Policy Contract about making good choices for yourself. By signing and dating the Personal Policy Contract, it became an obligation to yourself that cannot be broken.

Unit 4

Commitment

Self-Management:
Understanding, Communicating and Assessing
Behavioral Competency, 3rd Edition
Gian Paolo Roma - © 2019 - All Rights Reserved

Understanding Commitment

"Commitment is an act, not a word."

~ Jean Paul Sartre

Our behavioral patterns communicate traits about the way we function, and those traits affect how others see us and how we see ourselves. Character traits are distinguishing features about our nature. These traits create lasting impressions in the minds of people who experience our behavior. One of the most important character traits an individual can communicate is commitment. Commitment is a trait that communicates an individual's …

willingness to follow through and meet obligations.

Commitment is an emotional and intellectual devotion to one activity over other activities. In general, if an individual is committed to an activity, he or she gives that activity more attention and time compared to other activities. The activity is treated as a priority and is moved to the front burner to meet its requirements. As Jean Paul Sartre explains in the above quote, commitment is an act and as such is communicated non-verbally. Words cannot do homework, show up to class, hammer a nail, build a bridge, play a violin concerto, or put a person on the moon. Only activity (actions and deeds) can do these things.

We can think about commitment related behavioral patterns as either *strengthening* or *weakening* trust, or *productive* or *unproductive,* respectively. *Productive* behavioral patterns such as showing up on time, working hard, and producing high-quality output, strengthen trust connections with the audiences that experience the behavior. *Unproductive* behavioral patterns such as lack of effort, being unreliable, poor quality output, and lack of accountability can weaken goodwill and cooperation and may require other people to step in to encourage more trustworthy performance.

Three commitment behavioral variables can be measured and analyzed to determine an individual's level of commitment to an activity. Figure 3-1 on the next page shows the three variables that demonstrate commitment: dependability, hard work, and work quality[33].

---

[33] Adapted from Kathryn Jackson's writings from two articles:

   i.   Response Design Corporation, Kathryn Jackson, "How to Set Performance Standards to Ensure Excellent Service", Product No. 10038, http://www.responsedesign.com/store/10038.pdf, also.

   ii.   Response Design Corporation, Kathryn Jackson, "Adapting Schedule Adherence Measurement to Improve Performance", Product No. 10038, http://www.responsedesign.com/store/10039.pdf.

Commitment Model

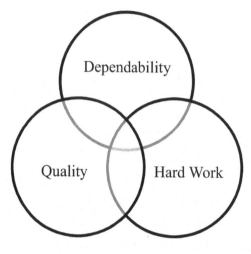

Figure 3.1

The Venn diagram demonstrates the overlapping relationship between the three commitment variables, which means that certain behaviors can affect all of the variables simultaneously. For instance, undependable behavioral patterns, like not showing up to class, may reveal problems with a student's work ethic and, at the same time, may be the cause of poor academic performance (quality).

Committed behavior is a function of being dependable, working hard, and producing quality output. Skill, with very few exceptions, is learned and a direct result of these three variables. In the same way that playing the violin is a learned skill, so too are reading, writing, language, mathematics, music, nursing, accounting, surgery, litigation, plumbing, masonry, carpentry, cutting hair, writing computer code, stand-up comedy, basketball, chemistry, and so on. And just as one cannot expect to play the violin at Carnegie Hall without commitment, one cannot expect to have acquired skill in any activity (academic, career, personal, or social) without commitment. High levels of skill suggest high levels of commitment, while low levels of skill imply low levels of commitment.

Let's look at the three commitment variables in more detail.

Understanding Dependability

"People count up the faults of those who keep them waiting."

~ French Proverb

The first and most essential component of committed behavior is dependability.

Dependability measures the …

the degree to which individuals can be relied on by others.

Dependability is a necessary condition for involvement in organized activities with others such as employment, committees, teams, and other social groups. Regardless of the size of the group, dependable behavior communicates commitment to group goals. Undependable behavioral patterns (behavior that is regularly self-absorbed and insensitive to others) actually destroys group cohesion. For this reason, dependability is the behavioral minimum for committed behavior and must be a *group goal*. Other group members cannot count on undependable people.

As shown in the Dependability Model below (Figure 3.2), dependability is a function of three behavioral variables: (1) Attendance, (2) Accountability, and (3) Contribution.

Dependability Model

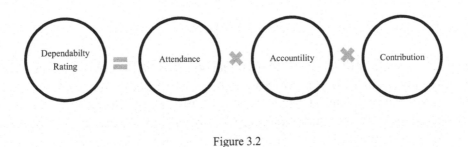

Figure 3.2

Each of these behavioral variables is required to be dependable and is made up of different sub-variables. If *any* of the variables (or their accompanying sub-variables) is low, the resulting *product* or dependability rating will also be low. For example, if a student consistently shows up to class but is consistently unprepared, he or she will not be perceived as being dependable.

Let's look at attendance, accountability, and contribution in more detail.

Attendance

To be dependable, one must first be in attendance. Comedian Woody Allen once said that, "Showing up is 80% of success." He wasn't joking.

To be in attendance is to be …

> **present (physically and mentally) at a specified place and time.**

Attendance involves three (3) variables: showing up, being on time, and staying put for the duration of the activity (Figure 3.3).

Attendance Model

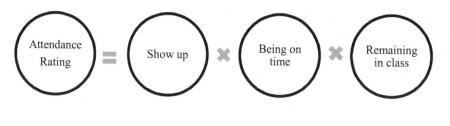

Figure 3.3

Although not showing up, tardiness, and leaving early are all different attendance-related issues, they all relate to being *present*. Being present is a function of being in attendance. One cannot be present if he or she is absent, late, or leaves early. Many students mistakenly believe that if they just show up to class they have attended the class. However, they cannot be considered present if they are not on time or leave early. Driving or walking to and away from class is not the same as being present in class. One is either present or not present.

Attendance is dependability's behavioral minimum. Failure to willingly and reliably show up on time, and remain in class for the duration of the activity would reveal problematic dependability-related behavioral patterns. One cannot *share responsibilities and support group goals* if he or she is not dependably present.

Accountability

The second variable in the dependability model is accountability.

Accountability is a …

> ***willingness to follow through and fulfill obligations.***

Accountability involves three (3) variables: responsibility, preparation, and readiness to perform (Figure 3.4)

Accountability Model

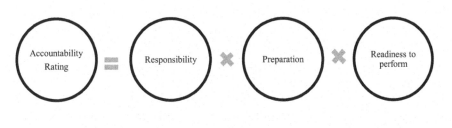

Figure 3.4

Accountability starts with being responsible.

Responsibility is …

> ***a palpable sense of duty about obligations to others.***

To explain responsibility, let's revisit the following scenario: After a hard day of work, three brothers are sitting on a couch with a big pile of laundry waiting to be folded. One of the brothers is responsible, one irresponsible, and the third's responsibility level is somewhere between the first two. How could we figure out who was who? The responsible brother would step forward and fold the laundry without having to be asked. The least responsible brother wouldn't fold the laundry even after being asked. The brother in the middle would fold the laundry, but only after being asked. Responsible people do what they are supposed to do without needing any guidance or prompting to do so. Irresponsible people don't do what they're supposed to do even after being asked.

Think About It

Do you fold your laundry without needing to be asked? If not, do you assume folding your clothes is somebody else's responsibility?

_____

_____

_____

_____

Next, to be ready to meet one's obligations, one must be prepared. Preparation is …

the process of becoming ready to perform.

Continuing with the laundry example … dinner cannot be ready if one is still preparing it. Readiness to perform is a function of preparation. Following this same logic, students cannot be ready for class or a test if they have not adequately prepared. Preparation requires a willingness to independently complete the work necessary to make oneself ready to perform. To be ready to perform students should willingly read all assigned materials, use the internet or tutors to supplement lecture and class materials, complete all homework and writing assignments, memorize key terms and formulas, rewrite notes. All of this requires a lot of time. Students who come to a test without preparing will not be ready to perform well on the test. In the words of legendary basketball coach John Wooden, Failure to prepare, is preparing to fail. Again, readiness to perform …

is a function of preparation.

Readiness to perform also requires having the proper tools to perform. Just as a carpenter cannot be ready to perform without having the proper tools (like a hammer), students cannot be ready to perform without books, calculators, paper, pencils, computers. … the tools of all knowledge workers. Failure to willingly and independently prepare oneself to be ready to perform indicates a lack of accountability for one's obligations. One cannot be viewed as dependable if he or she is not accountable.

Think About It

Imagine the following scenario. You are on a one-month group project for a particular class. The group project is worth 50% of your final grade. Each group member is responsible for specific parts of the project. You've had five one-hour group meetings. Every single team member showed up, on time, and stayed for the duration of each meeting. At the last meeting, the day before the project is due, everyone is supposed to hand in his or her work for inclusion in the final submission. At the meeting one of the team members announces, "I just started working on my section a couple of hours ago and I'm not ready, but here's what I've done so far."

Please explain how would you react if the group's project would not be ready to hand in? Does it matter that he or she had perfect attendance for every meeting? Why or why not? Please explain.

_____

_____

_____

_____

_____

_____

Contribution

The last dependability variable is contribution. One cannot be viewed as being dependable if one does not reliably contribute. Contribution measures the amount of …

value an individual brings to a group.

Although an individual's willingness to add value to a group may be affected by many trust-related issues, contribution is simply a function of three (3) variables: availability, involvement, and participation (Figure 3.5).

Contribution Model

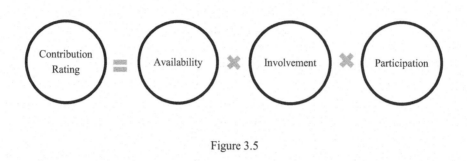

Figure 3.5

As discussed, contribution rating measures the amount of value an individual brings to groups. To add value to any group one must first make him or herself available to participate in group activities. Availability requires one to make time (scheduled or unscheduled) for group-related activities.

Availability is a measure …

of an individual's willingness to make time to support group goals.

Because nobody can be in two places at the same time, one is either available to participate or not. It's a black and white variable. Continuing with this logic, one cannot be involved in group-related activities if one is not available for group-related activities. So availability is a prerequisite for involvement and participation.

Involvement measures …

an individual's willingness to take on group responsibilities.

Individuals that take on more responsibilities within a group are more involved than individuals who do not. Some people think that being available is all that is required to make a contribution. Although they make themselves available, they are not actually involved in group activities. How can one contribute if he or she is unwilling to take on (or be responsible for) the work of the group? If an individual does not have a sense of duty about their obligations within a group, then he or she is nothing more than a warm body taking up space. One cannot meaningfully contribute if he or she is unwilling to be involved and do his or her fair share.

The last variable in the contribution model is participation. Participation is a measure of …

the effect an individual's involvement has on groups.

We can think theoretically of the effect of one's participation in groups as either *strengthening* or *weakening* group trust - or *healthy* or *unhealthy,* respectively. *Healthy participation* would strengthen trust and group connections and create goodwill between group members. Examples of healthy participation are showing up on time, working hard, appreciating others, and adapting to difficult or changing situations. *Unhealthy group participation* such as lack of effort and accountability, being unreliable, disrespecting others, using poor judgment, and making reckless decisions, can cause others to feel upset, frustrated, scared, and angry, which can destroy goodwill and cooperation in groups.

Participation is where all of the principles in this book are applied in the real world.

An individual's participation can have either a net positive or net negative contribution on group cohesion and trust. A positive contribution inspires confidence, while a negative contribution has the exact opposite effect. Individuals that violate attendance, accountability, or contribution principles communicate an unwillingness to meet their obligations to others. In short, they deprioritize their obligations, and in doing so, communicate that they cannot be trusted to perform their duties consistently. Undependable participation creates doubt in the minds of the people that experience it, which may cause them to act in a manner that safeguards their own interests.

Undependable behavior creates doubt that undermines trust.

Undependable people prioritize their own desires ahead of the interests, needs, and wishes of others. Try to keep that in mind as you make choices during your day. Even the most casual decisions, like choosing to sleep in instead of consistently showing up, being on time, or being ready to perform, can weaken your credibility and possibly even sever the trust that binds you to other people.

Self-Management:
Understanding, Communicating and Assessing
Behavioral Competency, 3rd Edition
Gian Paolo Roma - © 2019 - All Rights Reserved

Think about it

What are some behaviors that you consider particularly damaging to trust, goodwill, and group cohesion?

_____

_____

_____

_____

_____

In addition to trust, goodwill, and group cohesion, there are other very practical reasons why dependability is critically important. Dependable people are safer, more successful, less costly, and better team members than undependable people. Let's look at each of these byproducts of dependability, or lack there of.

Dependability and Safety

The first and probably most serious reason that dependability matters is safety. In some occupations, *not* consistently being prepared, available, or reliable can actually endanger the health and welfare of others. Firefighters, police officers, and members of the armed forces, all must trust their coworkers to be dependable when they go to work. Being undependable is a major ethical breach in these professions. If firefighters, police officers, or members of the armed forces are not dependable, they could seriously compromise the safety of everyone on their team.

Also, doctors, lawyers, nurses, paramedics, Red Cross workers, road crews, security guards, air traffic controllers, crossing guards, and pilots must be dependable or they could compromise the safety of people that depend on them. Below is an example of how quickly a situation can spiral out of control when an individual on a team is not dependable. The story is a personal account of what can happen when a co-worker is not dependable.

> When I was a patrol officer, there was another police officer who had recently been hired who had a reputation for not being dependable. I will refer to him as "Joe." On one occasion, I was dispatched to a bar fight. Serious injuries had already occurred. "Joe" was my backup officer. I arrived at the bar fight first. Unfortunately, the bar fight had spilled out into the parking lot, so I could not wait for my backup to arrive. As I

got out of my car, I heard the dispatcher continuing to call "Joe", but he did not respond. I continued anyway and in the process of breaking up the fight, I got hit a few times and stabbed.

Not until I got everything under control did Joe show up. As it turned out, Joe was busy away from his car socializing with a woman. The dispatcher finally got him on the radio and he "ran code red" all the way to the bar fight. But, it was too late. While I was stopping the fights, making the arrests, and heading to the emergency room, "Joe" was *earning* an undependable and untrustworthy reputation. [34]

Think about it

What specific dependability variables or rules did Joe violate? How would you react to Joe in the future? Explain.

_____

_____

_____

_____

_____

_____

Dependability and Success

The second reason why dependability is important is that it affects success. Being dependable influences one's success as a student and an employee. To try to understand how student dependability impacts academic success, I gathered attendance and grade data for all of the 206 students that completed my Accounting I, Accounting II and Human Resources Management courses over a 17-month period. The study only included students that received a final grade, and did *not* include students that withdrew before a final grade could be given. To gather the attendance data, I had students sign an attendance log at the beginning of every class. Table 3.1 below summarizes the findings of the study.

---

[34] Personal story of Greg Talley former Associate VP, Dean, and Professor at SUNY Broome Community College and Chief of Police in Los Alamos, New Mexico

Attendance	# of Students	% of Total	GPA	Average Grade
0 classes missed	47	24%	3.3	B+
1-4 classes missed classes	96	46%	2.8	B-
5-8 classes missed classes	32	15%	2.2	C
More than 8 missed classes	32	15%	1.2	D
Totals	*207*	*100%*		

Table 3.1

As the numbers show, there is a substantial correlation between final GPA and class attendance. Students with fewer absences received higher grades, while students with lower grades had higher absenteeism. In fact, students that did not miss any classes had 15% and 33% higher grades than students that missed 1-4 classes or 5-8 classes, respectively.

Attending class is one of the ways that students acquire knowledge. In class, professors introduce subject material, answer questions, explain homework, review for tests, and discuss their expectations. Outside of class, students are expected read their textbooks, complete assignments, and write papers. Students that consistently attended class were better prepared for tests.

Lastly, eleven percent of the students in this study received failing grades, and *none* of which were those with perfect attendance.

Think about it

Has your dependability affected your academic performance? Explain.

_____

_____

_____

_____

_____

_____

_____

Dependability and Cost

In an employment setting, undependable people are expensive to keep around. Prior to teaching, I was as a member of a wireless start-up company that is now part of T-Mobile, USA. My last position at the company was in customer service senior management. My department was responsible for, among other things, scheduling a 1000 plus person workforce at two 24/7 customer contact centers.

One of the most important variables we tracked in the department was how well customer contact representatives adhered to the schedules that we had given them. We tracked electronically when representatives were logged into the systems to take calls, how long they were logged into the systems, and how long they were logged out. Our goal was to achieve 90% schedule adherence. This meant that for an eight-hour shift, with 30 minutes for lunch and two 15-minute breaks, representatives should have been logged into the systems for 378 minutes each day. Our goal was to have all of our 1000 representatives logged into the systems, ready to take calls for a total of 1000 representatives x 378 minutes = *378,000 minutes* each day.

What we found was that our representatives were only adhering 80% of the time to their schedules, not the 90% we had budgeted for. This meant that all 1000 representatives were actually logged into our system ready to take calls for an average of only 336,000 minutes instead of the scheduled 378,000 minutes. The *42,000* minute difference in performance between scheduled to actual time meant that the company was paying for the equivalent of about *100 full-time equivalent employees* to show up and *not* work. If the average representative costs approximately $35,000 fully loaded cost (salary, benefits, etc) per year, the cost to the company of operating at 80% schedule adherence is *$3,500,000* per year ($35,000 x 100 representatives).

Think about it

What are some ways the company might address the dependability problem among its workers?

_____

_____

_____

_____

_____

_____

Dependability and Teamwork

Being undependable creates a lot more work for everyone else on a team. The work for firefighters, police officers, sales people, waitresses, construction workers, call center representatives, maintenance workers, dentists, manufacturing workers does not go away when people don't show up or are late, unprepared, or not ready to perform duties. The work is moved or shifted to dependable group members.

Imagine the following scenario. It's a hot and humid summer afternoon and you are the owner of an ice cream shop. There is a continuous line throughout the day of about 300 customers, but only two of three workers you had scheduled to work show up. The worker that did not come to work was a "no call, no show." Instead of servicing 300 customers between a team of three workers, you must now service all 300 customers between a team of only two. Without the third worker, customers wait longer for service, and some might get frustrated and leave the store, which would increase stress and frustration for the entire work team and hurt business.

Think about it

How would you react to an undependable person who increased your workload?

_____

_____

_____

_____

_____

I once had an employee who would call in sick from time to time. When we pulled his attendance log, which shows what days he missed for an entire year on one sheet of paper, we noticed that every few weeks he got sick on either Monday or Friday. What does the pattern tell you? Quick note: Many students also demonstrate this exact same dependability pattern in college.

Dependability Effectiveness: A Self-Assessment

Below Expectations	Meets Expectations	Role Model
Even with guidance, fails to provide evidence *(verbal, written, and behavioral)* that their actions and words are dependable and/or aligned with audience expectations.	With guidance, provides evidence *(verbal, written, and behavioral)* that their actions and words are dependable and aligned with audience expectations.	Independently provides evidence *(verbal, written, and behavioral)* that their actions and words are dependable and aligned with audience.
Even with guidance, fails to provide evidence that he or she can be relied on by others.	With guidance, provides evidence of these behaviors and can be relied on by others.	Willingly provides evidence of these behaviors and can be trusted and relied on by others.

Using the Behavioral Observation Scale below as a guide, for each statement on the following page write in the rating column the number corresponding to the degree to which you consistently exhibit the behavior described in the statement. Note, there are no right or wrong answers. All that is important is that you indicate how consistently you exhibit the behavior described in the action statement.

Use the following Behavioral Observation Scale:

---

5 = Almost always performs as described by the Role Model standard.

4 = Sometimes performs as described by the Role Model standard and sometimes perform as described by the Meets Expectations standards.

3 = Almost always performs as described by the Meets Expectations standard.

2 = Sometimes performs as described by the Meets Expectations standard and sometimes perform as described by the Below Expectations standards.

1 = Almost always performs as described by the Below Expectations standard.

	Action Statement	Rating
1	I attend all of my classes.	
2	I arrive on time to class.	
3	I remain in class.	
4	I don't look at my cell phone in class.	
5	I pay attention in class.	
6	I complete assigned homework prior to class.	
7	I prepare in advance for exams.	
8	I bring required materials to class including books, paper, computer, pencils, handouts, PowerPoints, completed/attempted homework etc.	
9	I ask questions that relate to the subject matter being discussed in class.	
10	I listen and try to make a positive contribution in class.	

Now transfer your answers for each statement into the corresponding space in the table below.

Dependability: Behavior Mapping Table

Item	5Cs	Variable	Behavior	Behavior Rating	Behavior Average
1	Commitment	Dependability	Attendance		
2	Commitment	Dependability	Attendance		
3	Commitment	Dependability	Attendance		
4	Commitment	Dependability	Attendance		
5	Commitment	Dependability	Attendance		
6	Commitment	Dependability	Accountability		
7	Commitment	Dependability	Accountability		
8	Commitment	Dependability	Accountability		
9	Commitment	Dependability	Contribution		
10	Commitment	Dependability	Contribution		
Average					

Average = $\sum$ of Behavior Rating/10: [ ]

Greater than 4: If your average is between 4 and 5, you are dependable, can be relied on by others, and require little guidance regarding your attendance, accountability, and/or contribution.

Between 3 and 4: If your average is greater than 3 but less than 4, with guidance you are dependable, but you usually require guidance regarding your attendance, accountability, and/or contribution.

Less than 3: If your average is less than 3, you are sometimes dependable, but occasionally even with guidance, you are not dependable.

Take your behavior averages for this section, calculate the new average of averages, and input that information into the Employability Profile on the following page.

Employability Profile   Student Name _____   Home School _____

Recommended for Employment [Select]	Total Work-Based Learning Hours [Select]	Portfolio Completed [Select]	Passed State/National Assessment [Select]
1	2	3	4	5

Below Expectations

Even with guidance, fails to provide evidence *(verbal, written, and behavioral)* that they communicate appropriately, prioritize important matters ahead of unimportant matters, show thoughtful concern for others, follow through and meet obligations, and adapt effectively to difficult, changing, and complex circumstances.

Even with guidance, fails to provide evidence of these behaviors and is unwilling to work on trust and responsibility.

Meets Expectations

With guidance, provides evidence *(verbal, written, and behavioral)* that they communicate appropriately, prioritize important matters ahead of unimportant matters, show thoughtful concern for others, follow through and meet obligations, and adapt effectively to difficult, changing, and complex circumstances.

With guidance, provides evidence of these behaviors and is willing to work on trust and responsibility.

Role Model

Independently provides evidence *(verbal, written, and behavioral)* that they communicate appropriately, prioritize important matters ahead of unimportant matters, show thoughtful concern for others, follow through and meet obligations, and adapt effectively to difficult, changing, and complex circumstances.

Willingly provides evidence of these behaviors and can be trusted with responsibility.

Where:

5 = Almost always performs as described by the "Role Model" standard.
4 = Sometimes performs as described by the "Role Model" standard and sometimes performs as described by the "Meets Expectations" standard.
3 = Almost always performs as described by the "Meets Expectations" standard.
2 = Sometimes performs as described by the "Meets Expectations" standard and sometimes performs as described by the "Below Expectations" standard.
1 = Almost always performs as described by the "Below Expectations" standard.

Communication
Trust a person to convey messages appropriately to others.
- Audience
- Involvement
- Message
- Evidence
- COMMUNICATION MEAN

Choices
Trust a person to prioritize important matters ahead of unimportant matters.
- Communication
- Commitment
- Coping
- Caring
- CHOICE MEAN

Commitment
Trust a person to follow through and meet obligations.
- Dependability — Attendance
- Dependability — Accountability
- Dependability — Contribution
- Hard Work — Time
- Hard Work — Deliberate Practice
- Hard Work — Delayed Gratification
- Hard Work — Effort — Energy
- Hard Work — Effort — Determination
- Hard Work — Effort — Stamina
- Quality — Measure of Excellence
- Quality — Continuous Improvement
- COMMITMENT MEAN

Coping
Trust a person to handle and adapt effectively to difficult, changing, and complex circumstances
- Coping — Change — Demonstration
- Coping — Adversity — Self-Awareness
- Coping — Adversity — Self-Restraint
- Coping — Adversity — Self-Improvement
- Coping — Complexity — Capability
- Coping — Complexity — Capacity
- COPING MEAN

Caring
Trust a person to show thoughtful concern for others.
- Caring — Consideration — Listening
- Caring — Consideration — Courtesy
- Caring — Consideration — Respectful
- Caring — Concern — Cooperation
- Caring — Concern — Helpful
- Caring — Concern — Compromise
- Caring — Conscientious — Thoughtful
- Caring — Conscientious — Careful
- Caring — Conscientious — Fair
- CARING MEAN

BEHAVIORAL COMPETENCY RATING (BCR) (MEAN OF MEANS)

Think about It

The Dependability Behavior-Mapping Table shows you if others can rely on you. What is your average? Can you be relied on? If not, why not?

_____

_____

_____

_____

Changing Habits

How can you employ Fogg's Behavior Model tiny habits described earlier to improve your level of dependability in college?

Please take a few moments and try to come up with one tiny dependability habit that you can use to help you become more dependable. As you think about changing your habits, think about framing the tiny habit in the following format suggested by Dr. Fogg: "After I (insert existing behavior), I will (insert new tiny behavior)."

After I _____,

I will _____.

Understanding Hard Work

"Nothing will work unless you do."

~ Maya Angelou.

The second variable in the commitment model is hard work. In tough economic times, it is easy to think that brains and talent alone create success. Although it may be true that innate talent and intelligence play roles in success, these traits are only precursors to success and need to be developed. Decades of research provide an overwhelming body of evidence that talent and intelligence are developed, and ultimately achievement and success, are attained through commitment and hard work.[35]

For a variety of political, technical, and economic reasons beyond the scope of this book, many of the low- and medium-skill jobs that once paid well and characterized America's economy have slowly been either automated or outsourced to countries with lower wages and salaries. In today's competitive global marketplace, employers in all types of fields are increasingly looking for employees that can use their knowledge, skills, and abilities (KSAs) to make organizations more efficient, effective, and competitive. They are searching domestically and internationally for people with highly developed KSAs that are a result of hard work. So what is hard work? We can define hard work as …

difficult mental or physical activity done to develop intelligence and talent.

Hard work has three defining characteristics: (1) time with deliberate practice, (2) delayed gratification, and (3) effort. As shown in the Hard Work Model below (Figure 3.3), the product of these variables equals the value of your work output.

Hard Work Model

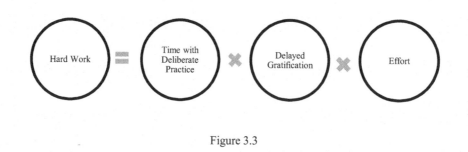

Figure 3.3

---

[35] Dweck,C.S., Mindset: The New Psychology of Success. New York: Random House. (2006).

Time with Deliberate Practice

My grandfather once told me that there are two kinds of people: those who work and those who take the credit. He told me to try to be in the first group; there was less competition there.

~ Indira Gandhi

Time gives us the ability to see the effects of our actions on our lives. One cannot become a first-rate doctor, musician, nurse, lawyer, writer, salesperson, computer programmer, mechanical engineer, artist without investing large amounts of time developing those skill sets. According to researchers …

time is a primary ingredient in developing skills.[36]

Research estimates that it takes about 2.7 hours per day every day for 10 years of practice to develop world-class expertise in any field. That's about 10,000 hours (the only exceptions to this rule are height, body mass, and quickness). This research sites a 1993 study that found that exceptional talent in music, mathematics, chess or sports required lengthy periods of instruction and practice.[37] The most exceptionally talented students put in a lot more time than less talented students. This research also found that it did not matter how talented the musicians were when they started. None of the elite performers were naturals who did not put in long hours of practice. The most talented people were not always naturally gifted when they started, or the smartest; they were the people who put in the most time and practice.

Research shows that the same concept also applies to knowledge-based skills such as mathematics, reading, and writing.[38] It takes time to learn how to read and write well. It takes time to become proficient in mathematics or a language. Although it helps to have great teachers, research shows that your own commitment to succeed is far more important than any other factor. Genuine skill development requires a real sacrifice of time.

---

[36] Anders K. Ericsson, Michael J. Prietula, Edward T. Cokely, "The Making of an Expert", *Harvard Business Review*, (July/August 2007).

[37] Anders K. Ericsson, Ralf T Krampe, Clemens Tesch-Römer,; "The role of deliberate practice in the acquisition of expert performance", *Psychological Review*, Vol 100(3), Jul 1993, p.363-406.

[38] Op Cit, Dweck (2006).

Investing time into developing yourself is particularly difficult when you think that you lack the requisite skills or ability for high levels of achievement. Practicing something that you are not proficient at requires much more concentration than practicing something that you excel at.[39] Researchers point out that deliberate practice entails …

"considerable, specific and sustained effort to do something you can't do well. It involves improving the skills you already have and extending the reach and range of your skills."[40]

For example, the best basketball players in the world can shoot and dribble with their right and their left hand. They can shoot the ball moving to the left and the right. They methodically and repeatedly practice every aspect of the game day after day, week after week, month after month, and year after year. They develop world-class basketball skills by systematically thinking through and practicing what they are good at, as well as what they are *not* good at. They continually work to improve *every* aspect of their game for years.

Because deliberate practice requires much more concentration, it is hard to do for long periods of time. One can only devote "a couple hours a day"[41] to deliberate practice because it requires so much focus. Nevertheless, people who are deliberate in their approach to skill development and hard work, practice a couple of hours every day for years. It all adds up. For example, if you practice writing every day for a couple of hours, you will total almost three thousand hours in just four years. Three thousand hours is enough time to become a good writer.

College is all about learning new subject matter. Some subjects you may be good at and some you may not. Some classes are more demanding than others. Sitting and staring at subject matter that you find difficult for hours on end is not productive. A better way is to concentrate for smaller amounts of time in a deliberate way. For some subjects involving problem solving, such as math, accounting, economics, or physics, the key is to know how to approach the problems. For students who are having difficulty with these types of classes, it may not be possible to do the work without a basic understanding of the logic and how the formulas work. To gain that understanding, deliberate practice might involve working with a tutor for a few hours every week to practice the formulas. After gaining a basic understanding of how to solve problems, deliberate practice might then involve doing problems repeatedly (a couple hours at a time) to reinforce the learning, or "teaching the material to another person." [42]

---

[39] Op Cit, Ericsson, Prietula, Cokely (July/August 2007).

[40] Op Cit, Sloboda, Davidson, Howe, Moore (May 1996).

[41] Ibid. Ericsson, Prietula, Cokely (July/August 2007).

[42] As stated in a conversation with Katherine Collette, (June 2017).

For courses that emphasize writing, whether essays, short stories, or research papers, basic writing skills will be required. A brilliant idea that is not written well will undermine the impact of anyone's work. If a student lacks the basic writing skills required for these courses, deliberate practice might involve working at a writing lab for an hour or two each day to learn how to approach writing assignments and how to write. Deliberate practice is not just spending four hours to produce a poorly written paper.

Because deliberate practice involves doing things that you are not good at, you will be doing things that make you feel uncomfortable, frustrated, or even scared. These feelings are natural. Anytime you do something outside of your comfort zone, you might feel unsure of yourself. In order to develop the skills you need to accomplish your goals, you must try as hard as you can to push yourself forward and cope with those feelings.

Think about it

Do you think that you are a good student (Yes or No)? _____

Now, consider whether your answer was based on the amount of time and deliberate practice that you have historically dedicated to your coursework. Does the amount of time and deliberate practice that you have spent reading, writing, solving math problems, doing homework, preparing for exams, learning a foreign language, learning an instrument have anything to do with your response? Please explain.

_____

_____

_____

_____

_____

_____

_____

_____

Delayed Gratification

"You cannot escape the responsibility of tomorrow by evading it today."

~ Abraham Lincoln

The next hard work variable is delayed gratification. According to researchers, people who are *unable* to delay gratification (or postpone pleasure), "have more behavioral problems, in school and at home," than people who have developed this ability. Problems of "low-delaying adults" cited in the research include lower SAT scores, trouble paying attention, difficulty with friendships, higher body-mass index, and problems with drugs and alcohol.[43]

High-delaying people postpone fulfillment and handle work and problems immediately.

Low-delaying people are more likely to procrastinate, which only magnifies tension and stress. The amount of work that needs to be done in a shorter time period may become insurmountable. This is particularly a problem in academia and learning. New and conceptually difficult subject matter requires a great deal of time and concentration and limits the quantity of material one can learn each day. For example, if it takes forty hours of deliberate practice to fully learn all of the material for a Calculus exam, it is almost impossible to learn that amount of material in one or two nights.

This is because the human brain functions in much the same way as the human stomach. You cannot starve yourself for three weeks and then eat three weeks worth of meals in one or two nights. Your stomach would not be able to digest so much food that quickly. The same is true for your brain. No matter how hard you try, your brain cannot concentrate on conceptually difficult work like writing or complex math for more than two or three hours in a day before shutting down.[44] Also, it is doubly hard to focus when you are feeling stressed because you have to meet a deadline.

Multitasking is one of the ways students procrastinate. A 2009 study found that young people between the ages of 8 to18 years old spent an average of 7 hours and 38 minutes each day multi-

---

[43] Harriet Nerlove Mischel, Walter Mischel, The Development of Children's Knowledge of Self-Control Strategies, Stanford University, *Society for Research in Child Development, Inc*, 1983.

[44] John A. Sloboda, Jane W. Davidson, Michael J. A. Howe, Derek G. Moore, "The role of practice in the development of performing musicians", British Journal of Psychology, Volume 87, Issue 2, pages 287–309, May 1996.

tasking with media.[45] Time spent multitasking with phones, computers, TV, music, video games, print, and movies increased by more than 1 hour and 19 minutes, a 19% increase since 1999. Because multitasking involves more than one activity, it requires some level of distraction from the primary activity. The main problem with distracted activity is that it reduces one's ability to concentrate, thus reducing comprehension. Texting while driving is a good example of why multitasking can be problematic.

Driving requires that you have real-time knowledge of what is happening on the road. Texting moves your attention away from controlling a motor vehicle to reading and typing words into a cell phone. Once attention is distracted, your ability to comprehend and react to what is happening on the road diminishes. The National Safety Council describes distracted driving as "any non-driving activity a person engages in that has the potential to distract a driver from the primary task of driving and increase the risk of crashing."[46] Multi-tasking, by definition, is distracted activity. The main problem with distracted activity in learning is that it reduces one's ability to concentrate, thus reducing comprehension. Three main types of distraction impact learning:[47]

1. **Visual**—taking your eyes off the learning material (reading, writing, lecturer).
2. **Manual**—taking your hands off the learning material (book, pencil, computer).
3. **Cognitive**—taking your mind off the learning material.

As you probably already know, procrastination is a hard habit to break. Delaying gratification is how hard working people avoid procrastination. By postponing these activities until after their work is done, they can more fully enjoy their leisure time.

---

[45] Victoria J. Rideout, M.A., Ulla G. Foehr, Ph.D., Donald F. Roberts, Ph.D., "Generation M2: Media In the Lives of 8- to 18-year-olds", *A Kaiser Family Foundation Study*, January 2010, p.2.

[46] Indiana Criminal Justice Institute, "*Distracted Driving*", http:// http://www.in.gov/cji/3553.htm.

[47] Ibid (List from distracted driving wording copy on http:// http://www.in.gov/cji/3553.htm).

Think about it

Developing the ability to do something well requires a lot of time. As you have seen, time is one of the most important ingredients in developing skills of any kind. To help understand how you use your time, please fill out the following worksheet. After calculating the time you spend on each activity, add the times together and they should come close to 168 hours, the total number of hours/week.

Time Worksheet
A Self-Assessment

ITEM	ACTIVITY	TIME
1.	Sleeping	
2.	School	
3.	Employment	
4.	Domestic (parenting, cooking, cleaning, shopping, dishes)	
5.	Leisure	
6.	Commuting	
7.	Exercising	
8.	Religious observance, volunteer work	
9.	Procrastination	
10.	Studying	
11.	Other, internet, TV, gaming, movies	
	TOTAL HOURS PER WEEK	168

Do you feel that you have enough time to accomplish your academic goals? If not, what could you give up, or spend less time doing to free up more time? Can you eliminate any obvious time-wasters to increase the amount of time you devote to your schoolwork? Remember that you should prioritize important matters before important matters.

_____

_____

_____

_____

_____

Effort

"Satisfaction lies in the effort, not in the attainment. Full effort is full victory."

~ Mohandas Gandhi

More than 2400 years ago Sophocles said, "Success is dependent on effort." This is still true today. It is through effort that difficult tasks are accomplished. The more difficult the work, the more effort one must expend. For example, demanding mental activities, such as writing and math, may require much more concentration and focus than less demanding activities.[48] Effort is the outward physical manifestation of hard work. It is what people see and hear. We communicate our willingness to expend effort in many ways. Effort can be defined as a …

directed exertion of will.

Effort has three defining characteristics: energy, determination, and stamina. As shown in the Hard Work Model below (Figure 3.4), the product of these variables equals effort.

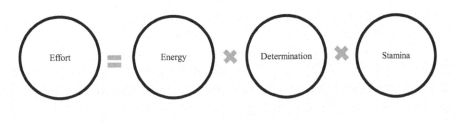

Figure 3.4

In his "Last Lecture," the late Randy Pausch eloquently described life as "a series of brick walls" that are put in front of people to keep those who don't want success badly enough *out*.[49] The lesson here is that your level of effort is visible to others. People who do not work hard may be considered by others to be lazy or undisciplined.

---

[48] Anders K. Ericsson, Ralf T Krampe, Clemens Tesch-Römer,; "The role of deliberate practice in the acquisition of expert performance", *Psychological Review*, Vol 100(3), Jul 1993, 363-406.

[49] Carnegie Mellon University, Randy Pausch Last Lecture: Achieving Your Childhood Dreams, https://www.youtube.com/watch?v=ji5_MqicxSo.

Energy

"The world belongs to the energetic."

~Ralph Waldo Emerson

Energy relates to the intensity of your resolve to accomplish work. If your energy level is high, your resolve to work hard is high and vice versa. A consistently high energy level communicates a high tolerance for work or desire to work hard, while a consistently low energy level communicates a lack of concern or lack of initiative to work hard. Although many things can affect your energy level in college, (e.g. the difficulty of the work, interest in the subject-matter) energy is simply a measure of the enthusiasm you bring to your schoolwork.

Determination

"Talent is nurtured in solitude. Character is formed in the stormy billows of the world."

~Johann Wolfgang von Goethe

Determination concerns the firmness of your resolve to complete work, especially when conditions become uncertain or difficult. Subjects that you find conceptually difficult or boring, perhaps organic chemistry, calculus, literature, or corporate finance may test your level of determination. Highly determined students will hang in there when the going gets tough. They persevere despite obstacles and setbacks. As the saying goes, "When the going gets tough, the tough get going." Less determined students might give up, withdraw, or even drop out of school when they face adversity. It takes a great deal of determination to hang in there when things don't go according to plan.

Stamina

"In the race for success, speed is less important than stamina"

~B.C. Forbes

The third variable in effort is stamina. Stamina relates to how long a person can persevere under difficult or challenging circumstances. The classic examples of people who possess stamina are marathon runners. Marathon runners persevere through pain and exhaustion to finish long and grueling races. Similarly, graduating from college requires that students remain firm and continue moving forward when conditions become difficult.

Studying for difficult exams and writing term papers requires that students put in time during which they may feel bored, tired, confused, and frustrated. Students with stamina have the ability to work through these negative emotions over long stretches of time to reach their academic goals. Some majors may require much more stamina than others depending on how challenging students find the material. Students who have difficulty with quantitative subjects such as math, physics, or economics will need more stamina to do well in those courses. Likewise, students who have a lesser aptitude for courses involving large amounts of reading and writing will need more stamina to achieve good results in those subjects.

Think about it

What does a grade point average communicate about student effort? Explain your answer.

_____

_____

_____

_____

_____

_____

_____

_____

_____

Understanding Quality

"Every job is a self-portrait of the person who does it. Autograph your work with excellence."

~ Unknown

What is a student? Students can be defined as self-employed knowledge workers who acquire and use knowledge to complete academic work assigned by educators. Students acquire knowledge by committing themselves to long periods of time reading, studying, attending lectures, deliberately practicing, and researching. Their primary job is to gain or attain knowledge and complete all academic work (assignments and tests) and to do so in a way that satisfies educator requirements. Therefore, academic quality is a measure of how well students meet the requirements of the educators reviewing their work. Quality is the …

outcome of committed behavior.

Educators use a variety of tools to assess the quality of student work including tests, quizzes, research papers, group projects, and oral presentations. Grades are measures of academic performance (residual evidence of the percentage of error-free academic work submitted by students). For example, a grade of 75% means that the work had an error rate of 25%. The error rate is the reciprocal of the grade. High grades mean low error rates, while low grades mean high error rates. What would your opinion be of a new car that did not start 25% of the time or a garbage man who hauled away only 75% of your trash or a waiter who got 25% of your order wrong? Would a 25% error rate be acceptable to you? In academia, a 25% error rate is passing. Grades are measures of academic quality. They are evidence of commitment — or your willingness to expend time and energy at the exclusion of other activities, to meet your obligations to professors. High grades reflect high levels of academic commitment, while low grades reflect low levels of commitment. Grades are measures of commitment.

Think about it.

How committed are you to your own education? How did you do in high school? What is your grade point average goal for college? Explain your answer.

_____

_____

Hard Work and Quality Effectiveness: A Self-Assessment

Below Expectations	Meets Expectations	Role Model
Even with guidance, fails to provide evidence *(verbal, written, and behavioral)* that their actions and words are appropriate and aligned with audience expectations.	With guidance, provides evidence *(verbal, written, and behavioral)* that their actions and words are appropriate and aligned with audience expectations.	Independently provides evidence *(verbal, written, and behavioral)* that their actions and words are appropriate and aligned with audience.
Even with guidance, fails to provide evidence of these behaviors and is unwilling to follow through and meet obligations to others.	With guidance, provides evidence of these behaviors and is willing to follow through and meet obligations to others.	Willingly provides evidence of these behaviors and can be trusted to follow through and meet obligations to others.

Using the Behavioral Observation Scale below as a guide, for each statement on the following page write in the rating column the number corresponding to the degree to which you consistently exhibit the behavior described in the statement. Note, there are no right or wrong answers. All that is important is that you indicate how consistently you exhibit the behavior described in the action statement.

Use the following Behavioral Observation Scale:

5 = Almost always performs as described by the Role Model standard.

4 = Sometimes performs as described by the Role Model standard and sometimes perform as described by the Meets Expectations standards.

3 = Almost always performs as described by the Meets Expectations standard.

2 = Sometimes performs as described by the Meets Expectations standard and sometimes perform as described by the Below Expectations standards.

1 = Almost always performs as described by the Below Expectations standard.

	Action Statement	Rating
1	I spend between 2 and 3 hours/night on homework, studying, or preparing for tests for every hour that I'm in class.	
2	I practice subjects more that I don't understand immediately.	
3	I seek out help from instructors, tutors, and study groups.	
4	I go out with friends only after my academic work is completed.	
5	I limit distractions or turn off phones, internet, TV, video games, print, movies while I am doing homework, studying, or preparing for tests.	
6	I have a level of energy to get my homework done, study, and prepare for tests.	
7	I have a "can do" attitude and seek help from tutors, teaching assistants, or professors immediately if I don't understand the material that I am learning.	
8	I hang in there and keep working hard for days, weeks, and months even when I don't understand something or when I don't get the grades I would like.	
9	I earn high grades (A's or B's) or marks in my classes.	
10	When I don't get the grades that I want I word harder and my grades improve.	

Now transfer your answers for each statement into the corresponding space in the table below.

Hard Work and Quality: Behavior-Mapping Table

Item	5Cs	Variable	Behavior	Behavior Rating	Behavior Average
1	Commitment	Hard Work	Time and Deliberate Practice		
2	Commitment	Hard Work	Time and Deliberate Practice		
3	Commitment	Hard Work	Time and Deliberate Practice		
4	Commitment	Hard Work	Time and Deliberate Practice		
5	Commitment	Hard Work	Delayed Gratification		
6	Commitment	Hard Work	Energy		
7	Commitment	Hard Work	Determination		
8	Commitment	Hard Work	Stamina		
9	Commitment	Quality	Measure of Excellence		
10	Commitment	Quality	Continuous Improvement		
Average					

Average = ∑ of Behavior Rating/10: ⬅

Self-Management:
Understanding, Communicating and Assessing
Behavioral Competency, 3rd Edition
Gian Paolo Roma - © 2019 - All Rights Reserved

Greater than 4: If your average is between 4 and 5, with little guidance you perform difficult mental or physical activity done to develop your intelligence and talent.

Between 3 and 4: If your average is greater than 3 but less than 4, with guidance perform difficult mental or physical activity done to develop your intelligence and talent.

Less than 3: If your average is less than 3, with guidance you sometimes perform difficult mental or physical activity done to develop your intelligence and talent., but occasionally even with guidance, you do not.

Take your behavior averages for this section, calculate the new average of averages, and input that information into the Employability Profile on the following page.

Recommended for Employment [Select]	Total Work-Based Learning Hours [Select]	Portfolio Completed [Select]	Passed State/National Assessment [Select]
1	2 3	4	5

Below Expectations

Even with guidance, fails to provide evidence *(verbal, written, and behavioral)* that they communicate appropriately, prioritize important matters ahead of unimportant matters, show thoughtful concern for others, follow through and meet obligations, and adapt effectively to difficult, changing, and complex circumstances.

Even with guidance, fails to provide evidence of these behaviors and is unwilling to work on trust and responsibility.

Meets Expectations

With guidance, provides evidence *(verbal, written, and behavioral)* that they communicate appropriately, prioritize important matters ahead of unimportant matters, show thoughtful concern for others, follow through and meet obligations, and adapt effectively to difficult, changing, and complex circumstances.

With guidance, provides evidence of these behaviors and is willing to work on trust and responsibility.

Role Model

Independently provides evidence *(verbal, written, and behavioral)* that they communicate appropriately, prioritize important matters ahead of unimportant matters, show thoughtful concern for others, follow through and meet obligations, and adapt effectively to difficult, changing, and complex circumstances.

Willingly provides evidence of these behaviors and can be trusted with responsibility.

Where:

5 = Almost always performs as described by the "Role Model" standard.

4 = Sometimes performs as described by the "Role Model" standard and sometimes performs as described by the "Meets Expectations" standard.

3 = Almost always performs as described by the "Meets Expectations" standard.

2 = Sometimes performs as described by the "Meets Expectations" standard and sometimes performs as described by the "Below Expectations" standard.

1 = Almost always performs as described by the "Below Expectations" standard.

Communication
Trust a person to convey messages appropriately to others.

	Audience
	Involvement
	Message
	Evidence
	COMMUNICATION MEAN

Choices
Trust a person to prioritize important matters ahead of unimportant matters.

	Communication
	Commitment
	Coping
	Caring
	CHOICE MEAN

Commitment
Trust a person to follow through and meet obligations.

	Dependability / Attendance
	Dependability / Accountability
	Dependability / Contribution
	Hard Work / Time / Deliberate Practice
	Hard Work / Delayed Gratification
	Hard Work / Effort / Energy
	Hard Work / Effort / Determination
	Hard Work / Effort / Stamina
	Quality / Measure of Excellence
	Quality / Continuous Improvement
	COMMITMENT MEAN

Coping
Trust a person to handle and adapt effectively to difficult, changing, and complex circumstances.

	Coping / Change / Demonstration
	Coping / Adversity / Self-Awareness
	Coping / Adversity / Self-Restraint
	Coping / Adversity / Self-Improvement
	Coping / Complexity / Capability
	Coping / Complexity / Capacity
	COPING MEAN

Caring
Trust a person to show thoughtful concern for others.

	Caring / Consideration / Listening
	Caring / Consideration / Courtesy
	Caring / Consideration / Respectful
	Caring / Concern / Cooperation
	Caring / Concern / Helpful
	Caring / Concern / Compromise
	Caring / Conscientious / Thoughtful
	Caring / Conscientious / Careful
	Caring / Conscientious / Fair
	CARING MEAN

	BEHAVIORAL COMPETENCY RATING (BCR) (MEAN OF MEANS)

Think about It

The Hard Work and Quality Behavior-Mapping Table shows you about your willingness to follow through and meet obligations. What is your average? Do you communicate commitment to the activities that you're involved in? If not, why not?

_____

_____

_____

Changing Habits

How can you employ Fogg's Behavior Model tiny habits described earlier to improve your level of commitment to college?

Please take a few moments and try to come up with one tiny commitment habit that you can use to help you improve your work ethic and academic quality. As you think about changing your habits, think about framing the tiny habit in the following format suggested by Dr. Fogg: "After I (insert existing behavior), I will (insert new tiny behavior)."

After I _____,

I will _____.

Important Terms

Do you understand the definitions of the following terms and phrases? Can you use each one correctly to describe your own behavior?

Participation
Attendance
Contribution
Commitment
Dependability
Participation
Involvement
Stamina
Quality
Delayed Gratification
Effort
Hard Work

Availability
Accountability
Responsibility
Dependability and Safety
Dependability and Cost
Dependability and Success
Dependability and Teamwork
Determination
Energy
Multi-tasking
Time
Deliberate Practice

Discussion of Meanings

1. Explain the three behavioral variables that demonstrate commitment.
2. In light of the discussion in this unit and in class, describe what commitment is, what it measures, and why it's important.
3. Define dependability and describe why it is important. Explain the three variables that demonstrate dependability.
4. Can people have good attendance, but not be considered dependable? Why or why not?
5. The contribution model is an evaluation of the value that individuals bring to groups. Contribution is a function of what three variables? Explain each variable.
6. Accountability is defined as a willingness to follow through and fulfill obligations. The accountability model involves three variables. Explain each variable and provide examples.
7. What is the most serious consequence of undependable behavior? Explain your answer.
8. Dependability is described as a teamwork goal. Why?
9. Why is undependable behavior expensive for organizations?
10. Explain the phrase, "Quality is the outcome of commitment." In your answer explain what quality means.
11. What is the primary ingredient of skill development? What is the main point the book and the class lectures make about skill development?
12. How does deliberate practice differ from practice?
13. Explain the marshmallow test.
14. Why is multitasking problematic for students?
15. What are the three variables associated with effort? Explain and provide examples of each.

Commitment Personal Policy Contract

To help you achieve your behavioral goals, you will be writing them down to create Personal Policy Contracts like the one below. By signing and dating the Personal Policy Contract, it becomes an obligation to yourself that cannot be broken.

Commitment Goals

Goals

Commitment goal(s) that will guide how I communicate in college:

_____

_____

_____

_____

Personal Policies

Personal policies I will follow about my levels of commitment:

_____

_____

_____

_____

Public Commitments

Public commitments that I will make to regularly measure how I am doing regarding my commitment goals and personal policies. I will send my goals, personal policies, and quick weekly progress reports to a supportive friend and the professor.

_____

_____

_____

_____

Signature: _____ **Date:** _____

Practice True/False Self-Test
(Explain if false)

Is each of the following statements *True* or *False*? Circle the best answer. If your answer is false, briefly describe why. (Hint: All of the answers are false)

For example:

1. The trust definition for Consideration is "Trust a person to show a thoughtful concern for others."

   True or *False*

   The answer is false because "Trust a person to show thoughtful concern for others" is the trust definition for Caring not Consideration.

---

1. The primary ingredient in skill development is ability.

   True or False

2. Deliberate practice and practice are essentially the same thing.

   True or False

3. Contribution is dependability's behavioral minimum.

   True or False

4. Procrastination is the same delayed gratification.

   True or False

5. Productivity is the outcome of committed behavior.   True or False

6. Deliberate practice is defined as difficult mental or physical   True or False
    activity done to develop intelligence and talent.

7. The (3) variables in the Effort Model are grit, sweat, and   True or False
    enthusiasm.

8. In addition to trust, goodwill, and group cohesion, the most   True or False
    important reason dependability is critically important is
    teamwork.

9. Dependability is a customer goal.   True or False

10. Attendance is a measure of the effect an individual's   True or False
    involvement has on groups.

To Sum Up

Unit 4 focuses on commitment.

First, the most important concept you learned in Unit 4 is that commitment is an act and as such is communicated non-verbally. Words cannot communicate commitment. You learned that commitment demonstrates your willingness to follow through and meet your obligations, and that an overwhelming body of evidence exists that indicates that talent and intelligence are developed through commitment.

Second, you learned that commitment is a function of three variables (dependability, hard work, and quality), and that certain behaviors can affect all of the variables simultaneously. Dependability was defined as the degree to which you can be relied on by others and is demonstrated by your attendance, accountability, and contribution to groups. Each of those variables was broken down further into sub-variables. You also learned that dependable people are safer, more successful, less costly, and better team members than undependable people.

Third, hard work was defined as difficult mental or physical activity done to develop intelligence and talent and is a function of three variables: (1) time with deliberate practice, (2) delay gratification, and (3) effort. Quality was defined as the outcome of committed behavior and is improved through dependability and hard work.

Fourth, you were asked to take dependability, hard work, and quality behavior self-assessments, and think about how tiny habits could help you improve your overall commitment.

Finally, to help you achieve your behavioral goals, you were asked to create a Commitment Personal Policy Contract for yourself. By signing and dating the Personal Policy Contract, it became an obligation to yourself that cannot be broken.

Unit 5

Coping

Self-Management:
Understanding, Communicating and Assessing
Behavioral Competency, 3rd Edition
Gian Paolo Roma - © 2019 - All Rights Reserved

Understanding Coping

"My dear,

In the midst of hate, I found there was, within me, an invincible love.
In the midst of tears, I found there was, within me, an invincible smile.
In the midst of chaos, I found there was, within me, an invincible calm.

I realized, through it all, that…
In the midst of winter, I found there was, within me, an invincible summer.
And that makes me happy. For it says that no matter how hard the world pushes against me, within me, there's something stronger – something better, pushing right back.

Truly yours,
Albert Camus[50]

The choices we make during times of difficulty, pressure, or strain shape the kind of people we become. Do we react before thinking? Do we let our emotions pull us in the wrong direction? Do we become critical of and blame others when we are stressed? Do we rationalize our behavior and poor decision-making? Difficult times test our ability to cope and in doing so shape our character. Helen Keller said, "Character cannot be developed in ease and quiet. Only through experiences of trial and suffering can the soul be strengthened, vision cleared, ambition inspired and success achieved."[51] Difficult situations create tension within us that can cause physical, intellectual, and emotional stress. There are always hard times. Coping is effective problem solving during difficult times. The process of coping with difficult situations builds character.

We can define coping as …

the ability to do the right thing during the most trying situations.

Yelling, getting upset, holding your breath, burying your head in the sand, turning your back on others, and jumping up and down are not coping strategies. Coping is the ability to effectively manage situations even when one is feeling infuriated, disrespected, frustrated, and scared. Coping effectively with mental anguish and worry involves real-time cognition at the time of a situation.

---

[50] Camus, A. (1942). *The Myth of Sisyphus*: *Essay Return to Tipasa*, Paris: Gallimard.

[51] Helen Keller (1880 - 1968) American Blind/Deaf Author & Lecturer.

One cannot cope with *now* after *now* has passed. Am I in control of my emotions in the present moment, or are my emotions in control of me? Individuals that cope well grasp the deep long-term moral significance of their decision making in real-time.

They are guided by an inner conviction to do what is "right," even when doing so involves sacrificing something that is highly valued. They have an inner "knowing" that doing the right thing is not an option because the alternative is an unending awareness of one's own moral shortcomings. Because we are at the center of everything that we do, we will know how we behaved and what we did *forever*. We cannot run away from our responsibilities to ourselves.

People define themselves and are defined by the decisions they make,
especially when the decisions are the most difficult to make.

Coping requires that we work outside of our comfort zones. Physical, intellectual, and emotional growth happens most profoundly when we solve problems and cope successfully with situations outside of our comfort zones. When we cope effectively with situations that are new, unfamiliar, or unpleasant, we extend the reach and range of our understanding of the world in ways that more familiar and comfortable situations cannot. How can individuals grow if they only do that which they already know how to do? Coping involves doing things that make us feel nervous or scared. These feelings are a natural part of coping. Any time you do something outside of your comfort zone, you can expect to feel unsure of yourself. To develop more fully though, you need to push forward despite those feelings.

Successfully coping with difficult situations and problems is the foundation upon which true self-trust and self-esteem are built. True self-trust is grounded in one's ability to cope successfully with the most difficult problems in one's life. Students who can cope with the physical, intellectual, and emotional challenges they encounter in college develop true self-trust.

Finally, the more situations people can cope with, the more value they bring to society. People with college degrees who can solve difficult and complex problems are in high demand in today's world. Doctors, nurses, lawyers, engineers (civil, mechanical, electrical), computer scientists, senior executives are all educated professionals that get paid well to solve specific types of problems. Remember, only about 30% of adults over the age of 25 years have a bachelor's degree or higher in the United States. The degree is evidence of and a testament to one's ability to cope.

In this unit, you will learn about coping with change, adversity, and complexity.

Understanding Change

"There is nothing permanent except change." [52]

~ Heraclitus of Ephesus

According to the Law of Change,[53] everything is continually in the process of becoming something else. Like death and taxes, change is impossible to avoid. Think about how the United States has changed over the last century. According to the U.S. Census Bureau, in 1910 the population of the United States was 92,407,000. As of May 2017, the population is around 325,146,337 and growing.[54] In 1910 only 13.5% of the population completed high school. Today, about 90% completes high school. In 1910, average life expectancy for men was about 48.4 years and women 51.8 years. Today, average life expectancy is about 75.6 years for men and 80.8 years for women. In 1910, Georgia, Missouri, Indiana, and Michigan had larger populations than California. Today, California's population is larger than all of those states combined. What will life be like in the year 2110?

It is hard to say for sure how the world will change, but we can say with certainty that it will change. If the world around us is changing, everyone should know how to cope with the problems and challenges associated with change.

Why can change be so difficult for people? Change is challenging because it forces people to cope with life outside of their comfort zones. To cope, one must be willing to accept or be patient with new and unfamiliar people, places, and activities. This push towards the unfamiliar can be hard for many people and can make them feel uncomfortable, even scared. That's because people often are generally more comfortable and confident in their ability to succeed in familiar situations.

Think about it. When you operate within your comfort zone, and the people, places, and activities are familiar and predictable, it is usually much less stressful than when the people, places, and activities are unfamiliar or unpredictable. It takes courage to face the unknown. For some people, it may take a while before they can summon up enough courage to deal with their fears and embrace change. They may resist change if they sense that it will force them out of their comfort zones. In psychology, the term for this is *status quo bias*.[55]

---

[52] Heraclitus of Ephesus, (540BC-480BC) Greek philosopher

[53] Jack M. Balkin, "The Laws of Change - I Ching and the Philosophies of Life", Sybil Creek Press, 2009.

[54] Citation, United States Census Bureau, https://www.census.gov/popclock/.

[55] Kahneman, D.; Knetsch, J. L.; Thaler, R. H. (1991). "Anomalies: The Endowment Effect, Loss Aversion, and Status Quo Bias". Journal of Economic Perspectives 5 (1): 193–206.

To better understand what happens to new students psychologically and emotionally when they experience status quo bias, a colleague asks new students a simple question, "What do you like better - variety or routine?" Many choose variety. Variety is fun and exciting. It is the spice of life. Routines, on the other hand, can be dull and mundane. However, when asked to look around and notice where everybody is sitting week after week, they observe that everyone usually sits in the exact same seat. Some students even get upset when someone is sitting in *their* usual chair. People may seek variety for some things - food, music, and restaurants - but people often cling tightly to their basic routines.

Routines are the familiar ways individuals perform their daily rituals and chores. They help us to process repetitive daily activities more efficiently. Like cruise control, routines make life easier by taking the thinking out of doing the recurring things that we do. Individuals form routines over time, and, like habits, they can be very difficult to break. College will interrupt many of your routines, and no matter how beneficial college may be for you, you should expect to feel uneasy because you will be giving up your old way of doing things … your old routines. Your feelings can run the gamut from being a little nervous and concerned to full-blown anxiety. It's important to realize that these feelings are normal because you are giving up something that you value: the comfort and familiarity of your old routines.

To complicate matters further, you may not know anyone at school, which means that you won't know whom you can and cannot trust. Trust is built over time, so you should expect to feel mistrustful of the new people that you meet until you get to know them. When you combine feelings of uneasiness brought about by changes in routines with the lack of trust, you may feel a bit overwhelmed and may even say to yourself, "This isn't for me." Even the best students can expect to feel this at some point in college, and it may take a bit of time for those feelings to go away. These uncomfortable feelings may be a natural consequence of transitioning to college. Most students will be able to cope with these feelings as they make the transition to college, but some may not. They may not be emotionally or psychologically ready to make the transition to college.

Think about it.

Some students do not understand that many of their daily routines will need to change when they enter college. They bring their high school mentality into college and do the same things that they did in high school, because that's what they know. Please list below some of the ways college may change your routines.

_____

_____

Student Readiness for Change

As discussed earlier, entering college brings students face to face with unfamiliar people and situations that they need to cope with. Some will embrace the change immediately, and some will accept it over time, but others may never fully adjust.

The Department of Education estimates that 31.8 percent of college students leave school after the first year.[56] Many of these students do not return because they were unable or unwilling to cope with change. Although college costs, socio-economic inequalities, financial pressures, child care needs, and other factors can play a role, many students simply drop out because they do not cope well with the changes that college requires. They may not even realize that when making the transition to college, it is normal to feel uncomfortable, confused, and, at times, overwhelmed.

We can refer to the varying degrees of emotional and intellectual readiness that new students bring to college as change readiness or transitional readiness. To help explain student readiness for college, let us look at an adapted version (Figure 4.1) of the Beckhard/Harris change model.[57] The model shows that the three variables on the left-hand side of the expression must outweigh the perceived cost of the change in order for the student to transition well into college. If the product is less than the perceived cost to the student, then a student may not be ready to change.

Student Readiness For Change Model

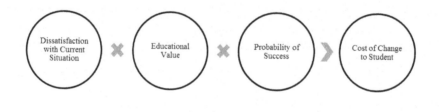

Figure 4.1

---

[56] National Student Clearinghouse, Snapshot on Persistence and Retention, First- Year Persistence Rate of College Students Declines, National Student Clearinghouse Research Center, May 2014, http://www.studentclearinghouse.org/about/media_center/press_releases/files/release_2014-07-10.pdf.

[57] Richard Beckhard, Reuben T. Harris, "Organizational Transitions: Managing Complex Change", *Addison Wesley Publishing Company*, 1987.

A student changes most readily when the product of the following situational elements are greater than the perceived cost of the change to the student:

1. his or her dissatisfaction level with current situation
2. how much the student values his or her education
3. the student's own perceived probability of success

If any of the variables on the left-hand side of the expression are low, student readiness decreases. For example, if a student were completely satisfied with his or her current situation, then the level of dissatisfaction would be zero. The product of anything multiplied by zero would, of course, be zero. Student costs may include physical and emotional tolls, financial expenses, disruption of current lifestyles, and opportunity costs. If any of the model variables on the left side of the expression are low, the chance for a successful transition to college is lowered significantly. Similarly, if the costs to the student are too high, there is also less of a chance of a successful transition.

Think About It

Please answer the following questions. (Circle Yes or No)

1. Are you dissatisfied with your current situation outside of school? (e.g. finances, work, home, friends, car.)   Yes or No

2. Do you see a direct benefit to you in getting a college education? (e.g. transfer or graduate schools, promotions, career.)   Yes or No

3. Do you think that you can be successful at college? (e.g. intellectual difficulty, balancing work and home obligations, financial, time, behavioral.)   Yes or No

According to the Beckhard/Harris Model, if you answered "No" to any of the above questions, you may need some time to make the transition to college. In the space provided below, please explain your "No" answers. What might you do to change these "No" answers into "Yes" answers?

_____

_____

_____

_____

Phases of Change

People are like stained-glass windows. They sparkle and shine when the sun is out, but when the darkness sets in, their true beauty is revealed only if there is a light from within.

~ **Elizabeth Kübler-Ross**

In 1969, Elizabeth Kübler-Ross first introduced the world to what happens when people receive news that they are fatally ill.[58] As you can imagine, this type of catastrophic news profoundly affects people, and stirs up intense emotional reactions. What Kübler-Ross found was the way that people react to this type of news is actually predictable. She said that people typically experience five emotional stages that are referred to as the 5 Stages of Grief: denial, anger, bargaining, depression, and acceptance.

Just try to image a doctor coming into your examination room. She closes the door behind her and says, "I'm sorry, but you have inoperable pancreatic cancer and you only have 6 months to live." How would you react? What Kübler-Ross said was that you would react in very predictable ways. She discovered that you may first be in denial. You might say to yourself, "This isn't happening to me." After some time passed, you might then move out of the denial stage and into the anger or bargaining phases. In these phases, you might become very angry and lash out at the world, or become scared, and try to negotiate or bargain with your God for clemency. After more time passed, and neither anger nor prayer worked to slow the progression of your illness, you might move out of the anger and bargaining stages, and slip into the depression stage. Finally, towards the end, you might want to make peace with the world, so you might grow to accept your fate.

Kübler-Ross's insights can also help explain how people will react to other, less traumatic changes or transitions that they experience. When new students enter college, many aspects of their lives could change. Their routines usually change, and they may not know anyone. In addition, they may be struggling financially and may not be confident academically. Having to cope with all of these changes, upheavals, and unknowns would make anyone feel anxious, confused, and even overwhelmed. It may be especially difficult for young people who are stepping out into the world by themselves for the first time.

We can use the Kübler-Ross model to help explain what happens to many students psychologically and emotionally when they enter college.[59] But instead of using the denial, anger, bargaining, depression and acceptance terminology used in the original model, we will simplify the model using only four terms to describe the typical ways that students react to college: *denial, destruction,*

---

[58] Elizabeth Kübler-Ross, "On Death and Dying," *Scribner*, 1969.

[59] The Kübler-Ross model is widely used in business and change management and there are many variations and adaptations of the model that help predict and manage behavioral reactions to change.

discovery, and demonstration. For our purpose, we can call this the 4 Stages of Student Grief Model (see Figure 4.2) on the next page.

4 Stages of Student Grief Model

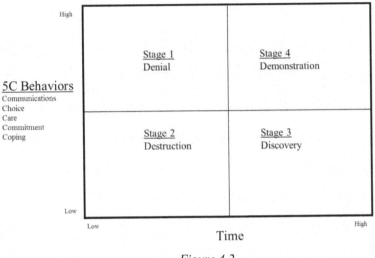

Figure 4.2

As Figure 4.2 shows, the 4 Stages Student Grief Model is a four-quadrant model that can serve as a conceptual framework for understanding what happens to many students when they enter college. Each quadrant represents a particular way students might react to college. When students come into college, they can react in one of three predictable ways. They can either:

1. Accept the change and immediately go to *Stage 4* and demonstrate that they understand what is required of them in college. They walk the walk and talk the talk. They communicate appropriately, make good choices, commit to academic excellence, treat others with respect, and cope effectively with the rigors of college.

2. Accept change over time, which means they might initially behave in ways that are antithetical to their own academic interests. They might take time to cycle through some or all four of the four stages (denial, destruction, discovery, and demonstration). For a period of time, they might make poor choices and communicate inappropriately, appear less committed than they should be, appear indifferent or even antagonistic, and appear to be unable to cope effectively with what is required of college students. However, these students will make the behavioral adjustments necessary to end up in stage 4.

3. Reject college altogether and never adapt to the change.

Keep in mind that the stages can overlap, exist simultaneously, or be experienced out of order. With this model, we can actually predict how students will react to change, and see who is adjusting well and who is not. Let's look at each stage.

Stage 1 - Denial

Students in the *Denial* stage do not demonstrate much, if any, interest in learning. They typically act like none of the material being taught is important or applies to them. As they begin to realize that their old way of doing things doesn't work, they may begin to act in ways that are antithetical to the 5Cs. They might make poor choices about their levels of commitment and/or consideration, and may demonstrate signs that they aren't coping.

What types of behaviors would you see that would identify students who are in the denial phase? What would you hear and/or see?

_____

_____

_____

_____

Stage 2 - Destruction

Students in the *Destruction* phase actively resist the educational process. They behave in a way that communicates that they are not coping with what is required of a college student. They make poor choices and their levels of commitment and consideration fall dramatically. They behave in an antagonistic way and in doing so fail to accept or comply with accepted behavioral norms. They seem very unhappy. What types of behaviors might you identify in students who are in the destruction phase? What would you hear and/or see?

_____

_____

_____

_____

Stage 3 – Discovery

In the *Discovery* phase, students begin to realize that they can handle the work. They might experience some success, which will give them feelings of hope, confidence, and courage. They begin to cope and start to take risks in class. It is as if a light bulb turns on and they begin to see what is in the darkness. They have a higher level of commitment, consideration, and energy in class. They start to smile. What types of behaviors would you see that would identify students who are in the discovery phase? What would you hear and/or see?

_____

_____

_____

_____

Stage 4 - Demonstration

The final phase is *Demonstration*. In the demonstration phase, students know that they can cope with the rigors of college. They know what they need to do, and they demonstrate student success. They may start to help their fellow students and may already be thinking about next semester or life after college. They are purposeful, confident, committed, and considerate. What types of behaviors would you see that would identify students in the demonstration phase? What would you hear and/or see?

_____

_____

_____

_____

Think About It

If students don't move quickly into the Demonstration Stage, they may experience some difficulty making the transition to college. Do you see yourself in the Demonstration Phase? If you answered no, what is keeping you from moving immediately into Stage 4?

_____

_____

Understanding Adversity

"Nothing makes a person desire improvement like failure"

~ Chris Stocking

The job of being an effective college student has always been challenging. There have always been demanding professors, overly competitive students, financial problems, high tuition and book costs, complex subjects, unreasonable deadlines, too much material to memorize, lazy team members on group projects, illness, and so on.

Many students react negatively to the stress of college when things don't work out according to plan. They may stop going to class or stop doing their homework or even drop out rather than cope with the problems they encounter. The fact that only about 33% of the adult population in the United States over the age of 25 has a bachelor's and 42% associates degrees or higher respectively, is evidence of the difficulty of the undertaking.[60]

Ultimately, coping with life's trials and tribulations (whether in college or not) requires an understanding of and belief in oneself. Life is not all good or all bad. There are ups and downs that each of us experience. Every person will face painful hardships throughout his or her life that he or she *alone* must cope with. These hardships create stress within us that we must overcome if we are to move forward with our lives.

Coping with adversity is a process of consciously attempting to understand, manage, and/or tolerate the stresses in our lives.

To help us understand coping with adversity during stressful times more, let us look at the Self-Control Model shown on the following page (Figure 4.3). The Self-Control Model components are: self-awareness, self-restraint, and self-improvement. The model helps guide thinking and ehavior during stressful times, which can help put situations into perspective and ease the pain and stress associated with adversity.[61]

---

[60] Camille L. Ryan and Kurt Bauman, United States Census Bureau, Educational Attainment in the United States: 2015 - Population Characteristics By Current Population Reports Detailed Tables, https://www.census.gov/content/dam/Census/library/publications/2016/demo/p20-578.pdf

[61] Stress is an ordinary and brief reaction to adversity. Stress usually doesn't lead to serious long-term problems. Although you may have great insight into your own ability to manage the stressors in your life, there may be times when you want to seek advice from professionals (counselors, therapists, etc). If you suffer from long periods (weeks or months) of negative feelings (i.e. sadness, anger, irritability, fear, anxiety, helplessness, confusion, or embarrassment) it may be time to talk to a health care provider.

Self-Control Model

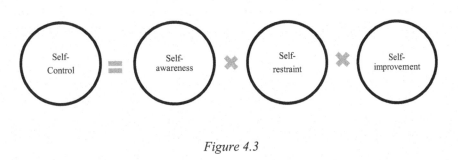

Figure 4.3

One is practicing self-control if one is:

1. aware of one's own desires, thoughts, emotions, and motives during stressful situations.
2. managing one's own behavioral reactions during stressful situations.
3. transforming over time one's own coping skills by one's own efforts during stressful situations.

If any of the variables on the right-hand side of the equation (Figure 4.3) are low, self-control decreases. For example, if a father slaps his 8-year-old son hard across the face because he didn't clean his room, the level of self-restraint of the father would be zero, and the product for his self-control would be zero as well. The product of anything multiplied by zero would, of course, be zero.

Like all of the other behavioral competencies in this book, the capacity to cope with adversity and stress varies among people and can be improved. But if a person does not willingly practice self-control by practicing self-awareness, self-restraint, and self-improvement, he or she is nothing more than a loose cannon. A loose cannon is a nautical term "for a cannon that breaks loose from its moorings on a ship during battle and has the potential to cause serious damage to the ship and its crew."[62] Not only can a loose cannon inflict grave damage on a ship, a person thought of as a loose cannon is "someone who behaves in an uncontrolled or unexpected way and is likely to cause problems for himself or herself and other people".[63]

---

[62] "Citation" Def. 1, https://en.wiktionary.org/wiki/loose_cannon.

[63] "Citation" Def. 1, http://dictionary.cambridge.org/us/dictionary/english/loose-cannon.

Self-Awareness

"That is the hardest thing of all. It is much harder to judge yourself than to judge others. If you succeed in judging yourself, it's because you're truly a wise man."

~ Antoine de Saint-Exupéry

None of us are as self-aware as we would like to be. We are all unique. Understanding our uniqueness, including our own behavior during difficult times, is an important part of developing a strategy for how to cope with problems you will face in the future. Are you usually good under pressure, or do you have a tendency to get angry, upset, or disengage in some way that may undermine your own effectiveness? Do you blame others when things go wrong? Do you take responsibility for your own actions? Without an accurate understanding of one's own predispositions (i.e., how we think and act during times of adversity), it is hard to cope with difficult situations effectively.

We can define self-awareness as …

an accurate understanding of oneself, including one's own desires, thoughts, emotions, and motives during difficult situations.

How can you make good decisions about how to react to a situation if you do not have a clear understanding of your own desires, thoughts, emotions, and motives? How would one know how to judge the appropriateness of his or her behavior if he or she did not have any standards for one's behavior? The ability to correctly prioritize matters during times of adversity requires self-awareness and behavioral understanding. It is at these times, at these decisive moments, when insightful self-awareness and appropriate behavioral action are most important. Without the understanding that accompanies self-awareness, clarity of judgment is very difficult.

Think about it

Take a few minutes and think about all of the possible stress inducing problems that college students can encounter. In the spaces provided on the next page, (1) list all of the problems that you can think of, (2) brainstorm as many possible reactions (good and bad) to each of problem that you came up with, and (3) try to identify any insights into your own reactions to stress inducing situations in college. Break down the insights into things you did or do well (strengths) and things you can improve.

(1) List the stress inducing problems that students face in college.

_____   _____

_____   _____

_____   _____

(2) List possible reactions (productive and unproductive) to each of identified problem.

Productive   ### *Unproductive*

_____   _____

_____   _____

_____   _____

(3) List insights about your own reactions to stress inducing situations in college.

Strengths   ### *Improvements*

_____   _____

_____   _____

_____   _____

In this exercise, we identified together stressful problems students face in college and a wide range of the productive and unproductive reactions to those problems. You were also asked to list any insights into your own reactions to problems that you face in college. In the same way that you were able to see productive and unproductive reactions to adversity and stress in others, they too can see your reactions. What will people see? Will they admire how you react to adversity and stress? Do you admire how you react to adversity and stress?

Years from now, if your family, friends, and associates are asked about your reactions to the problems that you faced in college, what would they say? If you believe that they will say that your reactions to problems were admirable, what evidence can you provide to substantiate your belief?

Self-Restraint

"The beauty of the soul shines out when a man bears with composure one heavy mischance after another, not because he does not feel them, but because he is a man of high and heroic temper."

~ Aristotle

Coping effectively with difficult situations (i.e. solving problems without hurting oneself or others in the process) communicates a great deal about your ability to handle pressure. Self-restraint helps take the emotion out of solving difficult problems, which makes it easier to clarify the nature and meaning of situations, and thereby improve reasoning and judgment. People that cope well with adversity, maintain their cool, when the going gets tough. They do not "throw a fit" every time something goes wrong in their life, and are able to maintain a calm and steady control over their emotions.

Self-restraint can be defined as …

the ability to successfully manage one's reactions during stressful situations.

Self-restraint requires you to work consciously through anxious feelings without acting on impulse, or behaving in angry or unreasonable ways towards others. Self-restraint is particularly hard when you are emotionally close to a situation. "True self-restraint is *keeping one's cool* when immediately affected by a situation."[64] Human beings are not machines. Each of us has lost our cool at one time or another and acted in incorrect, unwise, or unfortunate ways that we may regret. That is part of being human. When losing control of one's emotions is a standard way of behaving, patterns emerge that communicate a lack of proper regard for the needs, wishes, and feelings of others.

Self-restraint is good in almost every circumstance. It is a prerequisite for clarity of judgment when we are coping with important issues and making crucial decisions. Exercising self-restraint demonstrates that we have guiding principles or personal policies or mantras that inform our own behavioral decision-making during difficult times. Examples of personal policies or mantras for self-restraint might include, "I will try not to take things personally"; or "I will always try to maintain my composure when facing adversity"; or "I will never punch another person with my fists or my words." There are many others. Without defined standards for self-restraint, any behavior may appear to be okay. Without predefined personal policies, human beings are capable of great harm.

---

[64] As stated in a conversation with John Bunnell, November 2012.

Think about it

Are you in control of your emotions or are your emotions in control of you? Please take a few minutes to think about and write down your own set of self-restraint personal policies or mantras , which will help guide your behavior during difficult times.

Establish a zero tolerance personal policy for yourself regarding loss of self-restraint. Zero tolerance policies eliminate ambiguity that could cloud your judgment and decision-making during stressful times. For example, "It is *never* okay to pull the car over and attack another person" is an example of a self-restraint policy that provides clarity for behavioral options in times of extreme stress while driving. Physical assault is not an option in any setting, except perhaps in the most extreme of unsafe circumstances. A less dramatic "zero tolerance" policy might be, "I will always maintain my cool and not damage others, even when I am under pressure and things do not go my way." These policies remove the behavioral guesswork when confronted with difficult emotional situations. What are the types of self-restraint personal policies one might adopt in an academic setting?

Self-Restraint Personal Policies

_____

_____

_____

What do you think?

Stress reduction techniques can help you gain control of your emotions and reduce stress during difficult times. If you are stressed or angry, try the following breathing technique. It works.

Step 1	With your head straight, look up and close your eyes while still looking up.
Step 2	Inhale as deeply as you can four times. (Breath in through your nose slowly and out through your mouth, slowly)
Step 3	On the fourth breath, hold your breath for 5-10 seconds, and then slowly let your breath out.
Step 4	Sit still and then open your eyes after half a minute.

Self-Improvement

"The farther a man knows himself to be free from perfection, the nearer he is to it."

~ Gerard Groote

No one is perfect. Everyone has shortcomings that can be improved in some way. This is particularly true for coping. Coping with adversity is a difficult skill to master, especially when the adversity immediately affects you.

For our purposes, we can think about self-improvement as …

a life-long process of bettering one's own nature, abilities, and character by one's own efforts during stressful situations.

To improve coping skills, we must critically and honestly examine our own thoughts, emotions, behavior, and motivations *after* difficult events have passed. We need to continually evaluate our own behavioral performance against our personal policies and behavioral standards. This assumes that one has predefined standards against which their performance is measured. Was my behavior in alignment with my predefined behavioral standards, or did I fall short in some way? Without an honest evaluation of our own behavior following difficult times, we might not know if our approach to coping was effective.

Improving your ability to cope can be difficult due to the painful emotions and feelings that accompany tough times. For that reason, you need to have the emotional and intellectual strength to endure hardship, accompanied by the desire to improve your own reactions to adversity. Without a willingness to cope with difficult emotions, improving one's ability to cope with adversity is almost impossible. Life continually tests our ability to cope.

As my mother used to say, "You gotta wanna."[65]

Think about it.

Establish a self-improvement stretch goal for yourself in all matters. Stretch goals are long-term goals that you seek to attain. They can help clarify the rightness or wrongness of your thinking and behavior during times of adversity and stress and serve as an example or rule to live by. They

---

[65] Kari Bonini-Roma, *Artist and devoted mother of four children*, 1937-1996.

should be short and limited to one sentence (e.g., "I am committed to handling _all_ matters with grace or dignity").

In addition to identifying your self-improvement stretch goal, please identify the steps you think that you need to take to improve your coping skills. What are things you can do to improve how well you cope?

Self-Improvement Stretch Goal

_____

_____

_____

Improvement(s) needed to improve your coping skills

_____

_____

_____

_____

_____

_____

_____

_____

_____

Understanding Complexity

One of the primary responsibilities of students is to demonstrate that they can handle the complexity of college. Can you handle the workload required for each course? Can you handle the combined workloads for all of your courses? Do you have complete understanding of the course material, or has the course complexity hampered your comprehension in some way? Can you balance all of the academic and nonacademic activities you encounter in college?

Professors assess student academic work to determine whether their students understand and can cope with the level of academic complexity in their courses. Tests, quizzes, homework, oral and written reports, and class participation all measure the student's ability to cope with academic complexity. Most good professors will challange their students to determine how much complexity they can handle before they fall behind. Specifically, college stretches students to find out their capability (what students know) and capacity (how much academic and nonacademic work students can handle) levels.[66] (Figure 4.4)

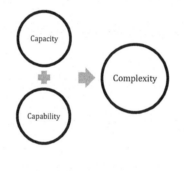

Figure 4.4

Capability

Capability is an assessment of one's ability to comprehend the academic and nonacademic world.

Is the level of comprehension complete, or is it incomplete? Capability is not solely a function of one's intellectual smarts. It is more than that. Good grades and academic understanding rely heavily on one's behavioral choices. Student behaviors, i.e. studying, showing up for class, putting

---

[66] Adapted from Joseph Cadwell, Leadership Skills for Managers: American Management Association, 2004, p.71.

in time to do homework, and delaying gratification, all influence student performance. Students who study and go to class learn more and perform better than students who do not.[67]

Academic capability relies on behavioral performance, and grades represent student proficiency in both areas (academic and behavioral). As discussed earlier, grades are measures of academic excellence, residual evidence of the percentage of error-free academic work submitted. In essence, grades are a measure of academic capability. For example, a 75% grade means that the student capably handled 75% of the questions, with an error rate of 25%. High grades mean highly capable, while low grades translate to a lower level of capability within that subject area.

One of the best ways to cope with courses that are difficult conceptually is to put together a workable plan to manage this complexity. A plan might include answers to the following questions:

- Can I space difficult classes out over several semesters so that I am not taking too many difficult courses at the same time?
- Can I take a course in the summer?
- When I do not understand something, how will I get answers to my questions?
- Is the professor approachable if I have questions?
- Can I use the Learning Assistance Department or get a tutor?

Capacity

Capacity is a measure of the quantity of academic and non-academic work a student can handle before their performance begins to erode.

Professors also assess student capacity. Textbooks are thick for a reason. Many textbooks and courses have content-rich vocabularies of technical terms. Every academic discipline has its own language. The languages may not be conceptually difficult to understand, but they may require learning many new terms.

When professors seem to be assigning too much work, they are trying to increase your capacity in their courses. Capacity, like capability, relies heavily on behavioral performance (i.e., putting in time and effort required to get through large quantities of subject matter).

---

[67] Gian Paolo Roma, Self-Management: Understanding Behavioral Competency, Createspace.com, 2014, Appendix I, p.40.

Think about it

Coping with the complexity (capability and capacity) of college requires behavioral competency. Take a few minutes and jot down some of the capacity and capability issues that you deal with at college.

Capacity Issues   **_Capability Issues_**

_____   _____

_____   _____

_____   _____

_____   _____

Have you been coping with the complex issues you face in college? Have you been putting in the time and effort required to cope with the complexity of college? If not, why not?

_____

_____

_____

_____

_____

_____

_____

Coping Effectiveness: A Self-Assessment

Below Expectations	Meets Expectations	Role Model
Even with guidance, fails to provide evidence *(verbal, written, and behavioral)* that their actions and words are appropriate and aligned with audience expectations.	With guidance, provides evidence *(verbal, written, and behavioral)* that their actions and words are appropriate and aligned with audience expectations.	Independently provides evidence *(verbal, written, and behavioral)* that their actions and words are appropriate and aligned with audience.
Even with guidance, fails to provide evidence of these behaviors and is unwilling to do the right-thing during the trying situations.	With guidance, provides evidence of these behaviors and is willing to do the right-thing during the trying situations.	Willingly provides evidence of these behaviors and can be trusted to do the right-thing during the trying situations.

Using the Behavioral Observation Scale below as a guide, for each statement on the following page write in the rating column the number corresponding to the degree to which you consistently exhibit the behavior described in the statement. Note, there are no right or wrong answers. All that is important is that you indicate how consistently you exhibit the behavior described in the action statement.

Use the following Behavioral Observation Scale:

5 = Almost always performs as described by the Role Model standard.

4 = Sometimes performs as described by the Role Model standard and sometimes perform as described by the Meets Expectations standards.

3 = Almost always performs as described by the Meets Expectations standard.

2 = Sometimes performs as described by the Meets Expectations standard and sometimes perform as described by the Below Expectations standards.

1 = Almost always performs as described by the Below Expectations standard.

	Action Statement	Rating
1	I am purposeful and committed to college.	
2	I get to class on time and stay put.	
3	I complete all of the work on time and am prepared for tests.	
4	I help other students when they are struggling with coursework.	
5	I am already planning for next semester and life after graduation.	
6	I notice my behavior and act in a manner consistent with my personal policies.	
7	I think before I react during difficult situations.	
8	I get proper perspective during difficult situations.	
9	I take the emotions out of difficult situations.	
10	I am patient with others and myself during difficult situations.	
11	I get my ego out of difficult situations.	
12	I value others and try not to judge during difficult situations.	
13	I don't take things personally during difficult situations.	
14	I am considerate to others during difficult situations.	
15	I am considerate even when I don't want to be during difficult situations.	
16	I don't blame others especially when I may have been the cause of a problem	
17	I accept responsibility for problems that I may have created.	
18	I apologize when necessary to those that I have harmed.	
19	I am honest with myself about my behavior.	
20	I understand and accept that difficult situations are a fact of life.	
21	I forgive others, for their behavioral missteps when I can.	
22	I complete my schoolwork without missing deadlines or sacrificing quality.	
23	I complete my home responsibilities without mismanaging other responsibilities.	
24	I juggle all of my responsibilities without getting too stressed.	
25	I don't schedule too many difficult classes during one semester.	
26	I space out my classes throughout the week to avoid overloading.	
27	I take difficult courses in the summer time to reduce complexity.	
28	I handle the conceptual difficulty of all of my classes.	
29	I talk to my professors when I struggle to understand subject matter.	
30	I use the Learning Assistance Department or a tutor when I need academic help.	

Transfer your answers for each statement into the table on the following page.

Coping: Behavior Mapping Table

Item	5Cs	Variable	Behavior	Behavior Rating	Behavior Average
1	Coping	Change	Demonstration		
2	Coping	Change	Demonstration		
3	Coping	Change	Demonstration		
4	Coping	Change	Demonstration		
5	Coping	Change	Demonstration		
6	Coping	Adversity	Continuous Self-Awareness		
7	Coping	Adversity	Continuous Self-Awareness		
8	Coping	Adversity	Continuous Self-Awareness		
9	Coping	Adversity	Continuous Self-Restraint		
10	Coping	Adversity	Continuous Self-Restraint		
11	Coping	Adversity	Continuous Self-Restraint		
12	Coping	Adversity	Continuous Self-Restraint		
13	Coping	Adversity	Continuous Self-Restraint		
14	Coping	Adversity	Continuous Self-Restraint		
15	Coping	Adversity	Continuous Self-Restraint		
16	Coping	Adversity	Continuous Self-Improvement		
17	Coping	Adversity	Continuous Self-Improvement		
18	Coping	Adversity	Continuous Self-Improvement		
19	Coping	Adversity	Continuous Self-Improvement		
20	Coping	Adversity	Continuous Self-Improvement		
21	Coping	Adversity	Continuous Self-Improvement		
22	Coping	Complexity	Capacity		
23	Coping	Complexity	Capacity		
24	Coping	Complexity	Capacity		
25	Coping	Complexity	Capacity		
26	Coping	Complexity	Capacity		
27	Coping	Complexity	Capability		
28	Coping	Complexity	Capability		
29	Coping	Complexity	Capability		
30	Coping	Complexity	Capability		
Average					

Average = ∑ of Behavior Rating/30: ⟵

Greater than 4: If your average is between 4 and 5, you cope well, and require little guidance to do the right thing during trying situations.

Between 3 and 4: If your average is greater than 3 but less than 4, it indicates that you cope well, but sometimes require guidance from others to do the right thing during trying situations.

Less than 3: If your average is less than 3, it indicates that with guidance you sometimes do the right thing during trying situations, but often fail to do the right thing even when advised to do otherwise by others.

Now take your behavior averages for this section, calculate the new average of averages, and input that information into the Employability Profile on the following page.

Employability Profile   Student Name _____   Home School _____

Recommended for Employment [Select]	Total Work-Based Learning Hours [Select]	Portfolio Completed [Select]	Passed State/National Assessment [Select]
1	2	3	4 5

Below Expectations

Even with guidance, fails to provide evidence *(verbal, written, and behavioral)* that they communicate appropriately, prioritize important matters ahead of unimportant matters, show thoughtful concern for others, follow through and meet obligations, and adapt effectively to difficult, changing, and complex circumstances.

Even with guidance, fails to provide evidence of these behaviors and is unwilling to work on trust and responsibility.

Meets Expectations

With guidance, provides evidence *(verbal, written, and behavioral)* that they communicate appropriately, prioritize important matters ahead of unimportant matters, show thoughtful concern for others, follow through and meet obligations, and adapt effectively to difficult, changing, and complex circumstances.

With guidance, provides evidence of these behaviors and is willing to work on trust responsibility.

Role Model

Independently provides evidence *(verbal, written, and behavioral)* that they communicate appropriately, prioritize important matters ahead of unimportant matters, show thoughtful concern for others, follow through and meet obligations, and adapt effectively to difficult, changing, and complex circumstances.

Willingly provides evidence of these behaviors and can be trusted with responsibility.

Where:

5 = Almost always performs as described by the "Role Model" standard.
4 = Sometimes performs as described by the "Role Model" standard and sometimes performs as described by the "Meets Expectations" standard.
3 = Almost always performs as described by the "Meets Expectations" standard.
2 = Sometimes performs as described by the "Meets Expectations" standard and sometimes performs as described by the "Below Expectations" standard.
1 = Almost always performs as described by the "Below Expectations" standard.

Communication
Trust a person to convey messages appropriately to others.

- Audience
- Involvement
- Message
- Evidence
- COMMUNICATION MEAN

Choices
Trust a person to prioritize important matters ahead of unimportant matters.

- Communication
- Commitment
- Coping
- Caring
- CHOICE MEAN

BEHAVIORAL COMPETENCY RATING (BCR) (MEAN OF MEANS)

Commitment
Trust a person to follow through and meet obligations.

- Dependability — Attendance
- Dependability — Accountability
- Dependability — Contribution
- Hard Work — Time
- Hard Work — Deliberate Practice
- Hard Work — Delayed Gratification
- Hard Work — Effort
- Effort — Energy
- Hard Work — Effort — Determination
- Hard Work — Effort — Stamina
- Quality — Measure of Excellence
- Quality — Continuous Improvement
- COMMITMENT MEAN

Coping
Trust a person to handle and adapt effectively to difficult, changing, and complex circumstances

- Coping — Change — Demonstration
- Coping — Adversity — Self-Awareness
- Coping — Adversity — Self-Restraint
- Coping — Adversity — Self-Improvement
- Coping — Complexity — Capability
- Coping — Complexity — Capacity
- COPING MEAN

Caring
Trust a person to show thoughtful concern for others.

- Caring — Consideration — Listening
- Caring — Consideration — Courtesy
- Caring — Consideration — Respectful
- Caring — Concern — Cooperation
- Caring — Concern — Helpful
- Caring — Concern — Compromise
- Caring — Conscientious — Thoughtful
- Caring — Conscientious — Careful
- Caring — Conscientious — Fair
- CARING MEAN

Think about It

The Coping Behavior-Mapping Table shows you about your willingness to do the right thing during trying situations. What is your average? Do you use good judgment during difficult situations? If not, why not?

_____

_____

_____

Changing Habits

How can you employ Fogg's Behavior Model tiny habits described earlier to improve how you cope with being in college?

Please take a few moments and try to come up with one tiny coping habit that you can use to help you cope better with change, adversity, and complexity. As you think about changing your habits, think about framing the tiny habit in the following format suggested by Dr. Fogg: "After I (insert existing behavior), I will (insert new tiny behavior)."

After I _____,

I will _____.

Important Terms

As a student, you should understand thoroughly the following words and phrases. Can you explain them and use them correctly?

Change
Status Quo Bias
Routines
Student Readiness for Change
4-Stages of Student Grief Model
Denial
Destruction
Discovery
Demonstration

Adversity
Self-Control Model
Self-Awareness
Self-Restraint
Self-Improvement
Complexity
Capability
Capacity

Discussion of Meanings

1. Why is coping important? What is the basic idea of coping?
2. Coping is described in the book as the ability to do the "right thing" during trying situations. What does doing the right thing mean?
3. Why is change so difficult for people? In your answer, explain how routines and status quo bias affect people's willingness to change.
4. When students enter college, many aspects of their lives change. Using the 4-stages of student grief model, briefly explain what might happen to students psychologically and emotionally when they come to college.
5. How does student dissatisfaction factor into a student's possible readiness for change?
6. According to the student readiness for change model, if a student does not value education, his or her willingness to complete college decreases. How can you tell if a student does not value education?
7. If students do not think that they can do college-level academic work, the probability that they will complete college decreases. What can students do to increase their academic confidence?
8. People that cope with adversity consciously attempt to understand, manage, and/or tolerate the stresses in their lives. To do this requires self-control. Explain the three elements of self-control discussed in the book.
9. Explain the three variables in the self-control model.
10. The book describes self-awareness as an accurate understanding of oneself, including one's own desires, thoughts, emotions, and motives during difficult situations. How can a lack of self-awareness affect our reactions to stressful situations?
11. Explain the similarities between change, adversity, and complexity.
12. What is the difference between capability and capacity?

Coping Personal Policy Contract

To help you achieve your behavioral goals, you will be writing them down and create Personal Policy Contracts like the one below. By signing and dating the Personal Policy Contract, it becomes an obligation to yourself that cannot be broken.

Coping Goals

Goals

Coping goal(s) that will guide how I communicate in college:

_____

_____

_____

_____

Personal Policies

Personal policies I will follow when I cope with difficult situations:

_____

_____

_____

_____

Public Commitments

Public commitments that I will make to regularly measure how I am doing regarding my coping goals and personal policies. I will send my goals, personal policies, and quick weekly progress reports to a supportive friend and the professor.

_____

_____

_____

_____

Signature: _____ **Date:** _____

Practice True/False Self-Test
(Explain if false)

Is each of the following statements *True* or *False*? Circle the best answer. If your answer is false, briefly describe why. (Hint: All of the answers are false)

For example:

1. The trust definition for Consideration is "Trust a person to show a thoughtful concern for others."   True or *False*

    The answer is false because "Trust a person to show thoughtful concern for others" is the trust definition for Caring not Consideration.

---

1. The Student Readiness for Change model was adopted from the work of Elizabeth Kübler-Ross.   True or False

2. The process of resisting change, even if it is a positive change, if doing so forces people out of their comfort zones is called homeostasis.   True or False

3. The four stages in the 4 Stages of Student Grief Model 4D Model are denial, defiance, depression, despair.   True or False

4. Self-Awareness can be defined as the ability to successfully manage one's reactions during stressful situations.   True or False

5. According to the Student Readiness for Change model, if a student is not dissatisfied with his or her current situation, their willingness to change would increase.

True or False

6. Surviving is a process of consciously attempting to understand, manage, and/or tolerate the stresses in our lives.

True or False

7. The Self-Control Model is made up of the following variables: self-knowledge, self-image, and self-help.

True or False

8. Complexity is an assessment of one's ability to comprehend the academic and nonacademic world.

True or False

9. Commitment is the ability to do the right thing during the most trying situations.

True or False

10. Self-awareness is the ability to successfully manage one's reactions during stressful situations.

True or False

To Sum Up

In Unit 5, you learned that coping communicates one's ability to deal with difficult situations, and for that reason, is characterized as the situation-based trust trait. We reviewed three situations that you should be able to recognize and cope with: change, adversity, and complexity.

In the change section, you learned how hard it is for people to change their routines. You learned that change forces people out of their comfort zones, which creates fear in people. You were introduced to the term status quo bias.

Second, you were introduced to two change models: the Student Readiness Change Model and the 4 Stages of Student Grief Model. You were asked to think about where you see yourself relative to each model.

Third, you also learned important behavioral qualities that enable people to communicate self-control: self-awareness, self-restraint, and self-improvement. You were asked to think critically about how you handle adversity in your life, and to write down some stretch goals to help guide your decision-making during challenging times.

Fourth, we discussed strategies to help you manage complexity in your life. Specifically, you learned the difference between how capable you are and the amount of capacity you can handle.

Fifth, you reviewed some Quick Tips for coping with change, adversity, and complexity.

Sixth, you were asked to take a coping effectiveness self-assessment, and think about how tiny habits could help you improve your coping skills.

Lastly, to help you achieve your behavioral goals, you were asked to create a Coping Personal Policy Contract for yourself. By signing and dating the Personal Policy Contract, it became an obligation to yourself that cannot be broken.

Unit 6

Caring

Understanding Caring

"Love of truth shows itself in this, that a man knows how to find the value and good in everything." [68]

~Johann Wolfgang von Goethe

When individuals interact with each other, they form connections. The connections can be strong or weak depending on the nature of the interactions. The context of the interactions affects the connections and defines the roles of the people involved and how they participate. Participation can range from warm, friendly, and sincere, to unfriendly, antagonistic, and disingenuous. This is true for interactions with family, friends and coworkers, as well as cashiers, customer service personnel, on-line help, police officers, professors, and anyone else. Regardless of the context in which individuals interact, conduct and attitudes that undermine another person's dignity, confidence, and self-worth will always weaken or possibly even sever the connections that bind people together. Interpersonal exchanges connect one person to another. Caring exchanges strengthen connections, while uncaring exchanges weaken connections. Why is this important?

For 75 years Harvard University has tracked the lives of 724 men about their work, home life, and health. The Harvard Study of Adult Development is the longest research project of its kind in history. [69] What the long-running study found is that the most important predictor of whether we age well and live a long and happy life is not wealth, fame, and fortune we amass. "The most important indicator of long term health and well-being is the strength of your relationships with other people … family, co-workers, friends, relatives, and spouses." [70] Dr. Robert Waldinger, the Director of the Harvard Study of Adult Development study, points out that the study uncovered three big lessons about relationships with others. [71]

1. Social connections with others are good for our health, and loneliness is bad for us.
2. The quality of our relationships is more important than the quantity of our relationships. The difference between good and bad relationships depends on trust. People that could not confidently rely on others during times of adversity were less happy and had poorer health.
3. Good relationships with others protect brain functioning and memory.

---

[68] Goethe, Wolfgang von, "Maxims and Reflections", 1833

[69] Citation Harvard Study of Adult Development Website: http://www.adultdevelopmentstudy.org/.

[70] TEDx Talks. "The Good Life|Rober Waldinger|TEDxBeaconStreet". YouTube video 14:44. Posted (Nov 30, 2015). https://www.youtube.com/watch?v=q-7zAkwAOYg.

[71] Ibid, Waldinger, Youtube video.

According to Dr. Waldinger, "The good life is built with good relationships." Good relations with others start with being interested in the well-being of others. If an individual communicates (verbally or nonverbally) that he or she does not care about another's well-being, then the other party is not likely to care in return. Although not rocket science, many intelligent and well-educated people do not seem to grasp this basic concept.

Caring behavior is crucial in situations that depend on cooperation between people because it makes cooperative relations between people possible. Alexander Graham Bell once said, "Great discoveries and improvements invariably involve the cooperation of many minds." Bell understood that one individual working alone could not invent and manufacture a light bulb, land on the moon, or build an aircraft carrier. One individual cannot possess all of the knowledge, skills, and abilities or master all of the competencies required to complete undertakings such as these. However, thousands of individuals working together cooperatively over time have made possible the seemingly impossible. If Bell's insight into the importance of cooperation is accurate, and uncaring behavior destroys people's willingness to cooperate, then it is vitally important for people to understand what caring behavior is and is not.

Caring can be defined as …

a thoughtful concern that strengthens trust with others.

To help us understand what caring behavior is, let us look at the Caring Model shown in (Figure 5.1). In order to be viewed as caring, individuals should be (1) considerate, (2) concerned, and (3) conscientious in their interactions with others.

Caring Model

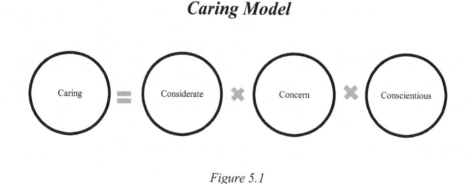

Figure 5.1

As discussed previously, behavioral patterns can be either *productive* or *unproductive*. Productive behavioral patterns, such as being nice, reliable, and compromising, strengthen trust connections because they communicate concern for others. While *unproductive* behavioral patterns, such as not listening, being rude, and not compromising, weaken trust connections because they communicate a lack of proper regard for others.

Let's look at the Caring Model in more detail.

Consideration

Caring behavior starts with being considerate. We can define consideration as …

Concern for the needs and feelings of others.

Considerate people: (1) listen, (2) are courteous, and (3) kind.

Consideration Model

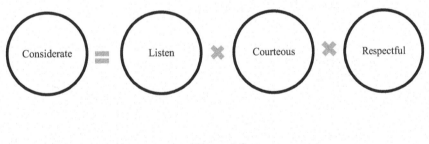

Figure 5.2

Consideration is caring's behavioral minimum. If a person is unwilling to listen, be polite, and/or be kind towards another, he or she is communicating that the other person is not worthy of respect. Not listening, being impolite, and being disrespectful is by definition inconsiderate behavior.

The main problem with inconsiderate behavior towards others is that it weakens or destroys cooperation and goodwill in people. Individuals who are treated poorly will show little, if any, willingness to assist or engage with inconsiderate people.

Let's look at the elements of consideration in more detail.

Listen

"Listen or thy tongue will keep you deaf."

Native American Proverb

Considerate people pay attention and listen to what others are communicating. Their focus is outward leaning. Making an effort to listen in an interested way is not a hovering attentiveness; it is a predisposition to appreciate authentically the opinions and ideas of others. Considerate people try to grasp the significance of alternate (or opposing) points of view because they understand how much they themselves may not know. Considerate people understand that no one has all of the answers, even if they are really smart, really articulate, and well-educated. Or as a colleague of mine asks, "Are you listening or waiting to talk".[72]

Inconsiderate people do not pay attention or listen to others, or make an effort to understand what other people are saying. Their lack of interest stifles goodwill and cooperation among people. They communicate that what others are saying is not worthy of their time. Inconsiderate people close off the connections that bind people together by disregarding the opinions and ideas of others as unimportant, irrelevant, or untrue.

Quick Tips For Becoming a Better Listener:

Be Attentive: Focus your mind, ears, and eyes on the people with whom you are interacting.

Don't Interrupt: Let people finish talking before you start talking.

Ask Questions: Ask questions to show interest, find out more, or if you do not understand what is being said (verbally and nonverbally).

Stay on Topic: Don't change the subject; it implies a lack of interest in what is being said.

Be Patient: Think long-term instead of short-term. Healthy, trusting relationships with others may take a while.

---

[72] As written by Brian Loy, May 2017

Reply Back: Provide verbal and nonverbal feedback to let the speaker know you understand and are interested in what is being said.

Courteous

"Really big people are, above everything else, courteous, considerate and generous -- not just to some people in some circumstances -- but to everyone all the time."

~ Thomas J. Watson

You cannot be viewed as considerate if you are not polite. Courteous people are well mannered and are aware of how their behavior affects others. They try to avoid harm in their interactions with others. Courteous people wait, hold the door for others, use turn signals when changing lanes, say "bless you" when someone sneezes, or "thank you" when a waitress brings their food. They take the time to acknowledge respectfully the presence of others. "Life be not so short but that there is always time for courtesy," Ralph Waldo Emerson reminds us.

Inconsiderate people, on the other hand, are rude and impolite. They ignore, snub, denigrate, humiliate, or embarrass other people. They are deliberately hurtful and insensitive to the feelings of others, and create situations where others feel upset, angry, or embarrassed. Discourteous people make others feel unworthy of their respect.

Think About It

What are three examples of impolite behavior that you notice in others? Please briefly describe below.

1. _____

2. _____

3. _____

Respectful

"What is objectionable, what is dangerous about extremists is not that they are extreme, but that they are intolerant. The evil is not what they say about their cause, but what they say about their opponents."

~ Robert F. Kennedy

Respect is demonstrating a regard for the feelings, rights, or traditions of others, not just people that think, act, and look like you. Respectful people are approachable and empathetic and acknowledge others in a friendly and good-natured way. They are decent people and do not require anything in order to be demonstrate decency towards others, even if they are the opposition. Rumi put it best when he said, "Whoever acts with respect will get respect."

While considerate people are respectful when they interact with others, inconsiderate people are insensitive and may treat others harshly. They are mainly concerned with their own desires, interests, needs, and wishes, and tend to ignore the feelings of others. People who are treated unkindly may experience feelings of inadequacy, anger, hostility, and resentment. What can be gained by creating these feelings in others?

A former colleague of mine, who was an operations director at a major telecommunications company in California, once told me a story that illustrates how inconsiderate behavior poisons relationships.

> Two of my employees were arguing about a new corporate human resources policy. Although both of the employees reported to me, they were not on the same level. One of the employees was my assistant, and the other was an operations manager.
>
> I can't remember what exactly they were arguing about, but the exchange was very public and very heated. Before it got too ugly, my assistant stormed off to get the policy to figure out who was right and who was wrong. When he returned, he waved the policy and very publically scolded the manager in front of everyone in the office, "I just went to HR and they gave me the policy statement. It says exactly what I said. I'm right. "
>
> At that point, the manager said, "Okay, you're right" and went back to her office. After a few minutes, I called my assistant into my office and asked him what had happened, and he told me the details of the argument, and said that, "he was right." Then, I said, "You might have been right, but you're *dead* right. You're now dead to Marianne. Was it worth it?" He didn't understand what I meant.

I explained that Marianne could be his next manager, or evaluate his performance, or be on a hiring committee for a job that he may be interested in, or on a promotion committee. I continued to explain that although he might never report directly to Marianne, that she had influence on his position and if she was asked about what it was like to work with you she might not give you a good recommendation. She might not say anything, she might just roll her eyes, but her point would be made. I explained that opportunities could be lost for him because of this event and he'd never know why.

How do you think Marianne will react to you the next time you need to interact with her?

I hope being right was really worth it.

The moral of this story is that other people don't really care if *you* are right or wrong. They do care about how they are treated. If you are interested in establishing and maintaining healthy, trusting, long-term relations with others, you will be respectful. Relationships are more important than being right. The late Wayne Dyer put it this way, "in terms of improving relations with others, it's better to be nice than right."

The other important lesson in this story is to never publicly denigrate, or openly treat another person like they are unworthy of your respect. Although they may forgive you, they will never forget. The communication axiom to remember is: praise in public and criticize in private.

Think About It

Think of a recent interaction, (whether or not you were involved) in which you observed disrespectful behavior. What did you think of the person exhibiting the behavior? What reactions did you observe from others?

_____

_____

_____

_____

_____

Concern

Concern can be defined as …

interest in another's well-being.

We can try to understand concern by comparing the degree to which an individual shows concern for others versus concern for oneself (Figure 5.4).

Concern Matrix

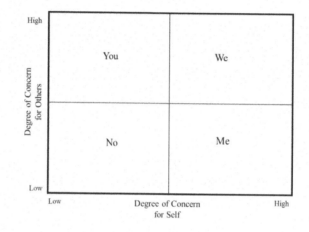

Figure 5.3

If people show a high degree of concern for others they communicate that they are interested in the wellbeing of others. As the grid shows, individuals that demonstrate a high level of concern for others have either a *"you"* or a *"we"* orientation. The distinction between "you" and "we" depends on the degree of concern the person shows for oneself.

A person that demonstrates a high degree of concern for others and a high degree of concern for oneself would be we-oriented. A we-oriented behavioral approach tries to balance one's own wants, needs, and desires with that of other people they interact with. In general, we-oriented individuals work hard at relationships and try to make sure that all parties (oneself and others) feel like they are treated fairly when interacting. By contrast, individuals with a "you" orientation would have high levels of concern for others, but low levels of concern for oneself. You- oriented individuals would subjugate their own needs to those of others.

Unconcerned behavior, which is at the other end of the Concern for Others spectrum, shows a low degree of concern for others, and is labeled on the chart as having either a no or a me orientation. The distinction between a no and me orientation would again depend on the degree to which the behavior shows concern for oneself. We can describe a no orientation as being indifferent or unconcerned about the outcomes of people's behaviors on themselves or others. In general, no-oriented people would view the outcomes of their own behavior as being an unimportant consideration in their dealings with others. Me-oriented people, on the other hand, would demonstrate a low level of concern for others, but a very high level of concern for themselves in their dealings with others.

What do you think?

What types of behaviors would people exhibit in the different quadrants? What quadrants do your associates, friends, and relatives fit into? What quadrant do you fit into?

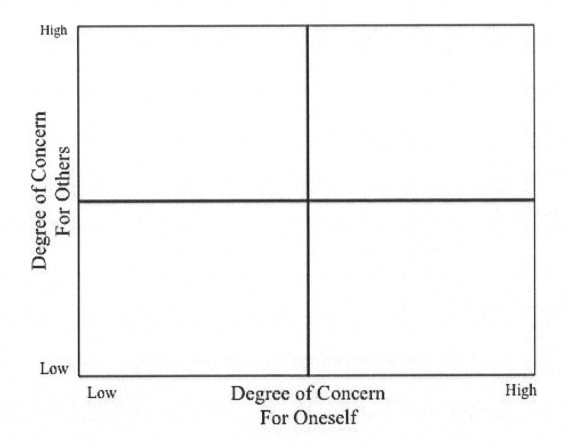

As you can see, concerned behavior is not a deep emotional understanding of another's feelings or problems. Rather, it is recognition that people have common interests that should bind us together. Without concern for others, *genuine* trusting relationships with others are not possible. As said throughout this book, everything you say and do communicates facts and information that influence how others see you. What and how we communicate helps others determine your underlying nature and whether they want to associate with you. Concern for others makes trusting, healthy, long-term relations with others possible.

Concern for others requires that people demonstrate that they are cooperative, helpful, and willing to compromise when it's appropriate to do so (Figure 5.4).

Concern Model

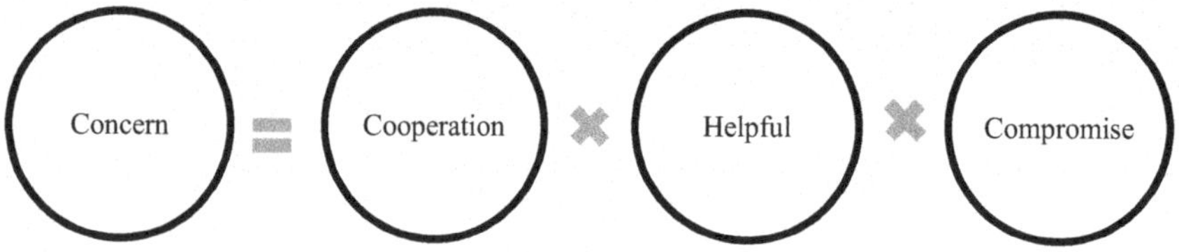

Concern = Cooperation ✖ Helpful ✖ Compromise

Figure 5.4

Let's look at each of these in more detail.

Cooperation

> *"Alone we can do so little; together we can do so much."*
>
> *~ Helen Keller*

When people cooperate they …

> ***willingly work together for a common purpose.***

The seventeenth century, John Donne said, "No man is an island". Nobody can have all of the knowledge skills and abilities required to complete massive undertakings such as landing on the moon or creating companies like Amazon, T-Mobile, and IBM by themselves. But thousands of people cooperatively working together did. We all rely on each other on the important work of survival done. The quality of our existence depends on the degree to which we can wort with and find common ground with others.

People that cooperate with each other willingly and openly interact and communicate with each other. They remain considerate when they reach impasses with others. It takes behavioral talent to build and maintain cooperation in others while interacting with others. As Lyndon Johnson reminds us, "There are no problems we cannot solve together and very few that we can solve by ourselves."[73]

When people communicate that they are *unwilling* to work with others cooperatively, they damage goodwill between themselves which can damage progress towards the achievement of goals. What good can come of this?

Helpful

> *"Look for the helpers. You will always find people who are helping."*

> *~Mr. Rogers*

Concerned behavior is helpful to others in need. Helpful people …

provide useful assistance to others.

To be helpful one should willingly provide support to others in ways that are appropriate. Helpful people are aware of and sympathetic to the plight of those around them. This helps create order.

Unconcerned behavior brings disorder and confusion to situations. Those who lack sensitivity to the feelings of people who need help, are unconcerned about the plight of those around them. They communicate that their personal needs and wishes are of paramount importance.

Think About It?

Everybody has household chores. There is cooking, cleaning, shopping, yard work, laundry, and garbage. In the space provided below, please list behaviors that you would define as being helpful and unhelpful.

---

[73] Lyndon B. Johnson: containing the public messages, speeches, and statements of the President (1965 edition).

Helpful	**Unhelpful**
_____	_____
_____	_____
_____	_____
_____	_____

Compromise

"If the contract is beneficial to both parties, it does not need to be written."

~Japanese Axiom

To the Greek dramatist Sophocles there was "no greater evil than men's failure to consult and to consider" each other.[74] Cooperative people compromise to settle disputes. They are concerned about everyone, not just people that think, act, and look like themselves. When people compromise with each other they …

willingly make concessions to settle disputes.

Cooperative people openly and sincerely engage in discussions aimed at reaching agreements that break roadblocks with others. When we compromise with each other, we demonstrate that we care about each other.

One way to demonstrate compromise, is to *"make sure everyone is happy"* at the conclusion of negotiated settlements. We can call this negotiating method *Murray's Rule*.[75] To follow Murray's Rule, both negotiating parties do whatever they can to make sure that the opposing party is treated

---

[74] ?496--406 bc, Greek dramatist; author of seven extant tragedies: Ajax, Antigone, Oedipus Rex, Trachiniae, Electra, Philoctetes, and Oedipus at Colonus.

[75] As state in a conversation with the late Murray Sanders, Spring 2004.

fairly during the negotiation. It's logical. If you show me that you care about what's important to me, I'll be more likely to care about what's important to you. Murray's Rule is we rather than me focused and uses caring behavior as a tool in negotiating. We-oriented negotiating is win/win, while me-oriented negotiating is at best win/lose, and at worst is lose/lose.

Quick Tips for Becoming a Better Negotiator:

- Keep in mind Murray's Rule. Know what is most important to you and try to figure out what is most important to the other party.
- Remain considerate to the other party by actively listening, being courteous, and concerned.
- Use disagreements with others as opportunities to practice negotiating. Problems you face with others are actually opportunities to develop negotiating skills that you will use throughout your life.
- Make offer statements or suggestions such as "How about if we …", or "What if we try …." if you are at an impasse.

Conscientious

"Management is not being brilliant. Management is being conscientious."

~ Peter Drucker

The last variable in the Caring Model is being conscientious. Conscientious people are thoughtful, careful, and fair in their dealings with others (Figure 5.4).

Conscientious Model

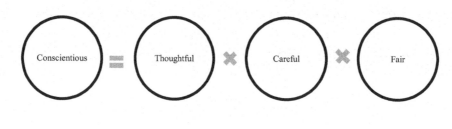

Figure 5.4

Conscientious people are …

guided by the dictates of their own thoughts and conscience.

They are ceaselessly aware of what is right and wrong about situations and their own behavior relative to each situation and to the standards that they have set for themselves. They are mindful about *all* of their interactions with other people. A person is conscientious if he or she is:

1. thoughtful or mindful when interacting;
2. careful not to demonstrate indifference when interacting; and
3. fair and reasonable when interacting.

Thoughtfulness, carefulness, and fairness all relate to the seriousness of one's intentions towards others and work. Conscientious people pay attention to the well-being and happiness of other people. To do otherwise, to be mainly concerned with one's own interests, at the exclusion of the interests of others, is to cause others to act in their own self-interest when dealing with you. How can this be good for you?

Think About It.

Using the same household chores discussed earlier (cooking, cleaning, yard work, laundry, garbage), please list behaviors that you would define as being conscientious and careless.

<u>Conscientious</u>   <u>Careless</u>

_____   _____

_____   _____

_____   _____

Quick Tips for the Caring Person

- Use polite phrases such as please, and thank you, or would you mind if we tried this …
- Ask meaningful questions.
- Practice patience, tolerance, and forgiveness, especially with those that you disagree.
- Limit your contact, if possible, with uncaring people (We all come into contact with such people at work, school, and elsewhere don't seek out these personality types).
- Be aware of your demeanor and tone, and avoid aggressive and dismissive behavior, especially with those that you disagree. It takes time to create understanding between people.
- Address people with a respectful tone, especially when you don't agree or feel upset.
- Be silent if you do not think you can say anything positive.
- Be constructive, non-confrontational, and don't get personal.
- Do not make generalizations or assumptions about a person's character.
- Make small goals for yourself. For example, if you get angry with another driver, imagine that the offending driver is rushing to the bedside of a dying loved one.
- Remember that arguing about religion and politics is similar to getting into an argument with a New York City cab driver … you won't win.
- Walk away when you're feeling like you are going to say or be disrespectful to another person.
- Show people that they are worthy of respect until they prove otherwise by being uncaring towards you, and then distance yourself and limit contact if you can.

Caring Effectiveness: A Self-Assessment

Below Expectations	Meets Expectations	Role Model
Even with guidance, fails to provide evidence *(verbal, written, and behavioral)* that their actions and words are appropriate and aligned with audience expectations.	With guidance, provides evidence *(verbal, written, and behavioral)* that their actions and words are appropriate and aligned with audience expectations.	Independently provides evidence *(verbal, written, and behavioral)* that their actions and words are appropriate and aligned with audience.
Even with guidance, fails to provide evidence of these behaviors and is unwilling demonstrate thoughtful concern for others.	With guidance, provides evidence of these behaviors and is willing to demonstrate thoughtful concern for others.	Willingly provides evidence of these behaviors and can be trusted to demonstrate thoughtful concern for others.

Using the Behavioral Observation Scale below as a guide, for each statement on the following page write in the rating column the number corresponding to the degree to which you consistently exhibit the behavior described in the statement. Note, there are no right or wrong answers. All that is important is that you indicate how consistently you exhibit the behavior described in the action statement.

Use the following Behavioral Observation Scale:

5 =   Almost always performs as described by the Role Model standard.

4 =   Sometimes performs as described by the Role Model standard and sometimes perform as described by the Meets Expectations standards.

3 =   Almost always performs as described by the Meets Expectations standard.

2 =   Sometimes performs as described by the Meets Expectations standard and sometimes perform as described by the Below Expectations standards.

1 =   Almost always performs as described by the Below Expectations standard.

	Action Statement	Rating
1	I focus my mind, ears, and eyes on the people with whom I am interacting.	
2	I let people finish talking before I start talking.	
3	I ask questions to show interest or if I do not understand what is being communicated (verbally and nonverbally).	
4	I don't change the subject when someone is speaking.	
5	I am patient and tolerant with people when I interact with them.	
6	I provide verbal and nonverbal feedback to let the speaker know I understand and am interested in what is being said.	
7	I use polite phrases such as please, and thank you, or would you mind if we tried this …	
8	I avoid doing harm when I interact with others.	
9	I take the time to respectfully acknowledge the presence of others.	
10	I ask people how they are doing.	
11	I inquire about what's going on in their life.	
12	I ask questions about things that others are interested in.	
13	I am available at times when people need assistance.	
14	I go out of my way to support others.	
15	I help create order when others need help.	
16	I use disagreements as opportunities to develop negotiating skills.	
17	I make suggestions such as "How about if we"…, or "What if we try" …. if I am at an impasse with another person.	
18	I know what is most important to me and try to figure out what is most important to the other party.	
19	I think about the impact of my choice of actions on others.	
20	I think about the impact of my choice of words on others.	
21	I think about the things that are important to others.	
22	I am careful not to offend others with my choice of actions.	
23	I choose my words wisely.	
24	I try to avoid potential problems with others.	
25	I am impartial in my dealings with others.	
26	I am reasonable when I interact with others.	
27	I am just when I make a decision about others.	

Caring: Behavior-Mapping Table

Item	5Cs	Variable	Behavior	Behavior Rating	Behavior Average
1	Caring	Consideration	Listening		
2	Caring	Consideration	Listening		
3	Caring	Consideration	Listening		
4	Caring	Consideration	Courtesy		
5	Caring	Consideration	Courtesy		
6	Caring	Consideration	Courtesy		
7	Caring	Consideration	Kindness		
8	Caring	Consideration	Kindness		
9	Caring	Consideration	Kindness		
10	Caring	Cooperation	Concern		
11	Caring	Cooperation	Concern		
12	Caring	Cooperation	Concern		
13	Caring	Cooperation	Helpful		
14	Caring	Cooperation	Helpful		
15	Caring	Cooperation	Helpful		
16	Caring	Cooperation	Compromise		
17	Caring	Cooperation	Compromise		
18	Caring	Cooperation	Compromise		
19	Caring	Conscientious	Thoughtful		
20	Caring	Conscientious	Thoughtful		
21	Caring	Conscientious	Thoughtful		
22	Caring	Conscientious	Careful		
23	Caring	Conscientious	Careful		
24	Caring	Conscientious	Careful		
25	Caring	Conscientious	Fair		
26	Caring	Conscientious	Fair		
27	Caring	Conscientious	Fair		
Average					

Average = ∑ of Behavior Rating/27:

Greater than 4: If your average is between 4 and 5, you are caring, show thoughtful concern for others, and require little guidance to do so.

Between 3 and 4: If your average is greater than 3 but less than 4, it indicates that you are caring, but sometimes require guidance to show thoughtful concern for others.

Less than 3: If your average is less than 3, it indicates that you sometimes show thoughtful concern for others, but occasionally fail to be caring even when advised to do otherwise by others.

Take your behavior averages for this section, calculate the new average of averages, and input that information into the Employability Profile on the following page.

Employability Profile   Student Name _____   Home School _____

Recommended for Employment [Select]	Total Work-Based Learning Hours [Select]	Portfolio Completed [Select]	Passed State/National Assessment [Select]
1	2	3	4	5

Below Expectations

Even with guidance, fails to provide evidence (*verbal, written, and behavioral*) that they communicate appropriately, prioritize important matters ahead of unimportant matters, show thoughtful concern for others, follow through and meet obligations, and adapt effectively to difficult, changing, and complex circumstances.

Even with guidance, fails to provide evidence of these behaviors and is unwilling to work on trust and responsibility.

Meets Expectations

With guidance, provides evidence (*verbal, written, and behavioral*) that they communicate appropriately, prioritize important matters ahead of unimportant matters, show thoughtful concern for others, follow through and meet obligations, and adapt effectively to difficult, changing, and complex circumstances.

With guidance, provides evidence of these behaviors and is willing to work on trust and responsibility.

Role Model

Independently provides evidence (*verbal, written, and behavioral*) that they communicate appropriately, prioritize important matters ahead of unimportant matters, show thoughtful concern for others, follow through and meet obligations, and adapt effectively to difficult, changing, and complex circumstances.

Willingly provides evidence of these behaviors and can be trusted with responsibility.

Where:

5 = Almost always performs as described by the "Role Model" standard.
4 = Sometimes performs as described by the "Role Model" standard and sometimes performs as described by the "Meets Expectations" standards.
3 = Almost always performs as described by the "Meets Expectations" standard.
2 = Sometimes performs as described by the "Meets Expectations" standard and sometimes performs as described by the "Below Expectations" standard.
1 = Almost always performs as described by the "Below Expectations" standard.

Communication
Trust a person to convey messages appropriately to others.

Audience	
Involvement	
Message	
Evidence	
COMMUNICATION MEAN	

Choices
Trust a person to prioritize important matters ahead of unimportant matters.

Communication	
Commitment	
Coping	
Caring	
CHOICE MEAN	

Commitment
Trust a person to follow through and meet obligations.

Dependability	Attendance	
Dependability	Accountability	
Dependability	Contribution	
Hard Work	Time	
Hard Work	Deliberate Practice	
Hard Work	Delayed Gratification	
Hard Work	Energy	
Hard Work	Determination	
Hard Work	Stamina	
Quality	Measure of Excellence	
Quality	Continuous Improvement	
COMMITMENT MEAN		

Coping
Trust a person to handle and adapt effectively to difficult, changing, and complex circumstances

Coping	Change	Demonstration
Coping	Adversity	Self-Awareness
Coping	Adversity	Self-Restraint
Coping	Adversity	Self-Improvement
Coping	Complexity	Capability
Coping	Complexity	Capacity
COPING MEAN		

Caring
Trust a person to show thoughtful concern for others.

Caring	Consideration	Listening
Caring	Consideration	Courtesy
Caring	Consideration	Respectful
Caring	Concern	Cooperation
Caring	Concern	Helpful
Caring	Concern	Compromise
Caring	Conscientious	Thoughtful
Caring	Conscientious	Careful
Caring	Conscientious	Fair
CARING MEAN		

BEHAVIORAL COMPETENCY RATING (BCR) (MEAN OF MEANS)

Think about It

The Caring Behavior-Mapping Table shows you about your willingness to demonstrate thoughtful concern that strengthens trust with others. What is your average? Do you communicate that you care about others? If not, why not?

_____

_____

_____

Changing Habits

How can you employ Fogg's Behavior Model tiny habits described earlier to demonstrate that you care about others?.

Please take a few moments and try to come up with one tiny caring habit that you can use to show that you care about people that you meet. As you think about changing your habits, think about framing the tiny habit in the following format suggested by Dr. Fogg: "After I (insert existing behavior), I will (insert new tiny behavior)."

After I _____,

I will _____.

Important Terms

As a student and citizen, you should understand thoroughly the following words and phrases. Can you explain them and use them correctly?

Caring
Harvard Study of Adult Development
Consideration
Listening
Courteousness
Kindness
Concern Model

Cooperation
Helpfulness
Compromise
Conscientiousness
Thoughtfulness
Carefulness
Fairness

Discussion of Meanings

1. Why is caring about others important to success?
2. The Harvard Study for Adult Development uncovered three big lessons about relationships. What were the lessons?
3. In light of what you have learned in this unit, explain why is caring behavior crucial in situations that depend on cooperation between people?
4. Being considerate is defined as concern for others. What are the three behaviors that demonstrate consideration? Explain each behavior.
5. Briefly describe the three behavioral variables that demonstrate that you care about others.
6. Explain and provide examples of each of the 4-quadrants in the Concern Model.
7. Why is concern for others so important to building trusting relations with others?
8. Do you know people that have a high degree of concern for themselves and a low degree of concern for others? What are some of the behaviors that would indicate that someone is "me" oriented?
9. What is Murray's Rule?
10. Why is it so difficult to forge trusting relations with others that do not compromise?
11. How can you tell if someone is cooperating?
12. Summarize some of the behaviors that demonstrate helpfulness.
13. Conscientiousness is described as being guided by the dictates of one's own thoughts and conscience. Explain the three variables that demonstrate conscientiousness.
14. The opposite of conscientiousness is careless. What are some of the behaviors that would demonstrate that someone is careless when they interact with others?
15. How would the world be different if people demonstrated that they cared for each other?

Caring Personal Policy Contract

To help you achieve your behavioral goals, you will be writing them down to create Personal Policy Contracts like the one below. By signing and dating the Personal Policy Contract, it becomes an obligation to yourself that cannot be broken.

Caring Goals

Goals

Caring goal(s) that will guide how I communicate in college:

_____

_____

_____

_____

Personal Policies

Personal policies I will follow when I am caring for others:

_____

_____

_____

_____

Public Commitments

Public commitments that I will make to regularly measure how I am doing regarding my caring goals and personal policies. I will send my goals, personal policies, and quick weekly progress reports to a supportive friend and the professor.

_____

_____

_____

_____

Signature: _____   **Date:** _____

Practice True/False Self-Test
(Explain if false)

Is each of the following statements *True* or *False*? Circle the best answer. If your answer is false, briefly describe why. (Hint: All of the answers are false)

For example:

1. The trust definition for Consideration is "Trust a person to show a thoughtful concern for others."

   True or *False*

   The answer is false because "Trust a person to show a thoughtful concern for others" is the trust definition for Caring not Consideration.

---

1. The three variables in the Caring Model are civility, concern, and conscientiousness.

   True or False

2. Caring is defined as a thoughtful concern that strengthens trust with others.

   True or False

3. Murray's Rule relates to being helpful.

   True or False

4. The three variables in the Consideration Model are listening, being courteous, and being kind.

   True or False

5. To improve relations with others, it is better to be right than nice.

    True or False

6. Consideration can be defined as a thoughtful concern that strengthens trust with others.

    True or False

7. Cooperation can be defined as interest in another's well-being.

    True or False

8. Conscientious people are not guided by the dictates of their own thoughts and conscience.

    True or False

9. The most important reason to demonstrate that you care about others is minimize conflict.

    True or False

10. A high degree of oneself and a low degree of concern for others is a "We" orientation.

    True or False

To Sum Up

In Unit 6 we defined caring as the convergence of three variables: consideration, cooperation, and conscientiousness. You learned the reason why consideration is characterized as the relationship-based trust trait and that good relations with others may not be possible without it. We also discussed why considerate behavior is particularly important for gaining cooperation from people.

You learned that in order to be viewed as caring, individuals should be considerate, concerned, and conscientious in their interactions with others. We broke down each of the caring variables into various sub-variable components.

Next, you were asked to describe some of the behaviors that would characterize the different levels of concern that people can have for others as (We, Me, You, No) orientations.

You were then asked to take a caring self-assessment, and to think about how tiny habits could help you improve how you care for others.

Lastly, to help you achieve your behavioral goals, you were asked to create a Caring Personal Policy Contract for yourself. By signing and dating the Personal Policy Contract, it becomes an obligation to yourself that cannot be broken.

APPENDIX I

Employability Profile

Self-Management:
Understanding, Communicating and Assessing
Behavioral Competency, 3rd Edition
Gian Paolo Roma - © 2019 - All Rights Reserved

Recommended for Employment [Select]	Total Work-Based Learning Hours [Select]	Portfolio Completed [Select]	Passed State/National Assessment [Select]
1	2	3	4

5

Below Expectations

Even with guidance, fails to provide evidence *(verbal, written, and behavioral)* that they communicate appropriately, prioritize important matters ahead of unimportant matters, show thoughtful concern for others, follow through and meet obligations, and adapt effectively to difficult, changing, and complex circumstances.

Even with guidance, fails to provide evidence of these behaviors and is unwilling to work on trust and responsibility.

Meets Expectations

With guidance, provides evidence *(verbal, written, and behavioral)* that they communicate appropriately, prioritize important matters ahead of unimportant matters, show thoughtful concern for others, follow through and meet obligations, and adapt effectively to difficult, changing, and complex circumstances.

With guidance, provides evidence of these behaviors and is willing to work on trust responsibility.

Role Model

Independently provides evidence *(verbal, written, and behavioral)* that they communicate appropriately, prioritize important matters ahead of unimportant matters, show thoughtful concern for others, follow through and meet obligations, and adapt effectively to difficult, changing, and complex circumstances.

Willingly provides evidence of these behaviors and can be trusted with responsibility.

Where:

5 = Almost always performs as described by the "Role Model" standard.
4 = Sometimes performs as described by the "Role Model" standard and sometimes performs as described by the "Meets Expectations" standard.
3 = Almost always performs as described by the "Meets Expectations" standard.
2 = Sometimes performs as described by the "Meets Expectations" standard and sometimes performs as described by the "Below Expectations" standard.
1 = Almost always performs as described by the "Below Expectations" standard.

Communication
Trust a person to convey messages appropriately to others.

	Audience
	Involvement
	Message
	Evidence
	COMMUNICATION MEAN

Choices
Trust a person to prioritize important matters ahead of unimportant matters.

	Communication
	Commitment
	Coping
	Caring
	CHOICE MEAN

BEHAVIORAL COMPETENCY RATING (BCR) (MEAN OF MEANS)

Commitment
Trust a person to follow through and meet obligations.

	Dependability	Attendance
	Dependability	Accountability
	Dependability	Contribution
	Hard Work	Time
		Deliberate Practice
	Hard Work	Delayed Gratification
	Hard Work	Effort
		Energy
	Hard Work	Effort
		Determination
	Hard Work	Effort
		Stamina
	Quality	Measure of Excellence
	Quality	Continuous Improvement
	COMMITMENT MEAN	

Coping
Trust a person to handle and adapt effectively to difficult, changing, and complex circumstances

	Coping	Change
		Demonstration
	Coping	Adversity
		Self-Awareness
	Coping	Adversity
		Self-Restraint
	Coping	Adversity
		Self-Improvement
	Coping	Complexity
		Capability
	Coping	Complexity
		Capacity
	COPING MEAN	

Caring
Trust a person to show thoughtful concern for others.

	Caring	Consideration
		Listening
	Caring	Consideration
		Courtesy
	Caring	Consideration
		Respectful
	Caring	Concern
		Cooperation
	Caring	Concern
		Helpful
	Caring	Concern
		Compromise
	Caring	Conscientious
		Thoughtful
	Caring	Conscientious
		Careful
	Caring	Conscientious
		Fair
	CARING MEAN	

APPENDIX II

Effect of Educational Attainment on Career Earnings and Employment

People entering the workforce without academic or technical proficiency are finding it more difficult to achieve their goals in today's increasingly competitive world. Decades of research have shown that over the course of their careers, college graduates are advantaged in two very important ways over their non-college counterparts: (1) they have much higher rates of employment, and (2) they earn much more money.

Let's first take a look at the relationship between educational attainment and rates of employment.

Education and Employment Rate

Each quarter, the U.S. Bureau of Labor Statistics publishes unemployment rate reports by educational attainment. The most current unemployment reports can be found in the footnote below.[76] What are the current national unemployment rates for the population 25 years and over by educational attainment? Please summarize your findings in the table below.

Educational Attainment	Unemployment Rate
Less than a high school diploma	
High school graduates, no college (1)	
Some college or associates degree	
Bachelor's degree and higher (2)	

(1) Includes persons with a high school diploma or equivalent.

(2) Includes persons with a bachelors, masters, professional, and doctoral degrees.

As you can see, the unemployment rate for well-educated workers is much lower than for workers with less education. That's because educational attainment is one of the most important factors used in making decisions about employment-related matters such as staffing and employee retention. This is particularly true in tight labor markets when unemployment rates are higher for all workers. When larger pools of well-educated workers are available to work, employers can be more selective in whom they hire and keep, which increases unemployment rates for less educated workers.

The relationship between educational attainment and employment can be found in a report published by the U.S. Census Bureau. The report describes how those with more education are

---

[76] Citation, United States Bureau of Labor Statistics, http://www.bls.gov/news.release/empsit.t04.htm.

more likely to work full-time, year-round than those with less education. To see for yourself, please go to and complete the following table.[77]

Educational Attainment	Employment Rate Full-Time, Year-Round Workers
None–8th grade	
9th–12th grade	
High school degree	
Some college	
Associate's degree	
Bachelor's degree	
Master's degree	
Professional degree (eg. engineer, lawyer, accountant)	
Doctorate degree	

What do you think?

If you were the owner of a company and you received 325 resumes for five job openings, how would you sort the resumes before you began reviewing them, and would you look at all 325 resumes?

_____

_____

_____

_____

_____

_____

---

[77] Citation: to http://www.census.gov/prod/2011pubs/acs-14.pdf, Education and Synthetic Work-life Earning Estimates Report: Table 1 (September 2011).

Education and Earnings

Although many factors affect how much money a person can make, one thing is clear: over a lifetime those with more education tend to earn a lot more money than those with less education. Education influences earnings in two ways: (1) as we have seen, people with more education spend less of their work-life unemployed, and (2) people with more education are in occupations that earn more money. According to the U.S. Census Bureau Report, "Education and Synthetic Work-Life Earnings Estimates" (2011):

> "Higher levels of education allow people access to more specialized jobs that are often associated with high pay. Degrees in many occupations are treated as job training that may be required for a position or earn the employee more pay within that position."

To see this for yourself, please go to and complete the table below with your findings which are footnoted below.[78]

Educational Attainment	Annual Earnings Full-Time, Year-Round Workers
None–8th grade	
9th–12th grade	
High School degree	
Some college	
Associate's degree	
Bachelor's degree	
Master's degree	
Professional degree	
Doctorate degree	

Source: Education and Synthetic Work-life Earning Estimates Report: Table 1 (September 2011)

Higher levels of education are required for many professions. Some jobs, such as lawyer, accountant, engineer, doctor, professor, and architect are impossible to get without the necessary educational credentials. Although there are no guarantees, a quick analysis of the data shows that for every year you invest in your education, the average return on the investment over a 40-year

---

[78] Citation: Education and Synthetic Work-life Earning Estimates Report: Table 1 (September 2011), http://www.census.gov/prod/2011pubs/acs-14.pdf.

working period is significant. Compared to the volatility of the stock and real estate markets, investing in your own education looks like a great bet.

What do you think?

If you owned a company, how would you determine how much each employee would be paid?

_____

_____

_____

_____

_____

_____

_____

_____

To sum up

The consequences of not attending or completing college can be harsh. Employers are increasingly looking for employees who can contribute in a meaningful way to their organizations. They are searching for people with knowledge, skills, and abilities that can add value to their bottom-lines.

Although there are alternatives to college for acquiring knowledge and developing skills, such as in technical and trade schools, a college degree remains a noteworthy achievement that society uses to make decisions about people. Many career opportunities are simply unavailable to those without a college degree. The degree is conclusive evidence that you have earned the opportunity to dine at their table. What you do with that opportunity will be up to you.

The next variable in making good choices is accurately assessing your own situation. (See Appendix II - "Reality Assessment" – on the next page.)

APPENDIX III

REALITY
ASSESSMENT

External Reality
Worksheet

Instructions:

In a group, brainstorm and write down some of the general trends (opportunities and threats) in the following External Reality Worksheet. External realities are opportunities and threats that exist outside of each person.

- Opportunities and threats are mostly beyond an individual's control and generally difficult to change. Although an individual cannot do much to change external reality, he or she can proactively figure out ways to deal with such conditions.

- Opportunities are favorable conditions that exist for pursuing educational or employment opportunities, such as more health care or accounting jobs.

- Threats are unfavorable conditions that could cause an individual trouble in college or career if not taken into account, such as the disappearance of low and medium skilled jobs that pay well. How will the external reality affect your situation over the next few years?

- Write down your collective responses in the worksheet on the next page.

External Reality
Worksheet

Opportunities (Favorable circumstances that are advantageous to you)	**Threats** (Unfavorable circumstances that could be harmful if you fail to consider them)

External Reality
Action Plan

Do any opportunities particularly appeal to you? What are the threats that most concern you? Please list the top opportunities, and the top threats that you believe will influence your own situation the most in the coming years. Then think about and write down what you need to do to take advantage of the opportunities and minimize the threats that you identify.

_____

_____

_____

_____

_____

_____

_____

_____

_____

_____

_____

_____

_____

Internal Reality
Worksheet

Instructions:

Working alone, write down as many things that you can think of that are distinctive about you on the *Internal Reality Worksheet* on the next page. Internal realities are your unique set of strengths and weaknesses that exist within you.

- Strengths are things we do well or that work in your favor, such as your behavior, computer, financial, math, writing, foreign languages, work ethic, musical, athletic.

- Weaknesses, on the other hand, are the things that may inhibit your ability to achieve your goals, such as lack of dependability, no marketable skills, lack of financial resources.

- To understand the role that your internal reality plays in your life, take a few minutes to jot down all the things you do well and things you may wish to improve.

Internal Reality
Worksheet

Strengths (Things you do well or that work in your favor)	**Weaknesses** (Things you don't do well or that inhibit your ability to do well)

What are your findings? What do you do well and where do you think that you need to improve? Are there ways that you can align your strengths with the opportunities that your group identified in the external reality worksheet? What are some strategies that you can employ to improve the areas of weaknesses that you identified?

_____

_____

_____

_____

_____

_____

_____

_____

_____

_____

_____

_____

_____

_____

About the Author

Gian Paolo Roma is Professor and Chair of Business Programs at SUNY Broome Community College in Binghamton, New York. He teaches management, accounting, and self-management courses, and lectures and consults on self-management and behavioral competency.

Prior to teaching and writing, Professor Roma worked for twenty years in the corporate sector at a variety of multinational and start-up companies. His last major corporate position was as a member of the start-up team that launched Omnipoint Communications, Inc., the first GSM wireless carrier in Northeastern United States (now part of T-Mobile). He headed up teams that launched Omnipoint's warehousing and distribution operation, regional marketing operations, and led the customer service strategy and planning department. Before being acquired, Omnipoint grew to over two thousand employees and one million customers in only 3.5 years.

Professor Roma started his career at UNISYS and Singer-Link in Quality Assurance Engineering, before working for Texaco (now part of Chevron) and NYNEX Mobile Communications (now part of Verizon Wireless) in Corporate Communications.

He has a BS in Industrial Technology from the Watson School of Engineering and Applied Science at the State University of New York at Binghamton, and an MBA from the Martino Graduate School of Business at Fordham University.

Publications:

Gian Paolo Roma, Self-Management: Understanding Behavioral Competency, First Edition, 5C Press, createspace.com, 2014.

Gian Paolo Roma, Self-Management: Understanding, Communicating, and Assessing Behavioral Competency, Second Edition, 5C Press, createspace.com, 2017.

Robert F. Hurley, Melissa Thau Gropper, Gianpaolo Roma, "The Role of TQM in Advertising: a conceptualization and Framework for Application", *Journal of Marketing – Theory and Practice,* Summer 1996, Vol. 4 No. 3.